GARETH O'CALLAGHAN

A Day Called Hope

A PERSONAL JOURNEY BEYOND DEPRESSION

HODDER

MOBIUS

Copyright © 2003 by Gareth O'Callaghan

First published in Great Britain in 2003 by Hodder and Stoughton
A division of Hodder Headline

The right of Gareth O'Callaghan to be identified as the Author
of the Work has been asserted by him in accordance with the
Copyright, Designs and Patents Act 1988.

A Mobius paperback

3 5 7 9 10 8 6 4

A CIP catalogue record for this title
is available from the British Library

ISBN 0 340 82648 7

Typeset by Hewer Text Ltd, Edinburgh
Printed and bound in Great Britain by
Mackays of Chatham plc, Chatham, Kent

Hodder and Stoughton
A division of Hodder Headline
338 Euston Road
London NW1 3BH

A Day Called Hope

'Any person capable of angering you becomes your master; he can anger you only when you permit yourself to be disturbed by him.'

– Epictetus

'The important thing is this: to be able at any moment to sacrifice what we are for what we could become.'

– Charles Du Bos

CONTENTS

ACKNOWLEDGEMENTS

Writing this book – my story – has been one of the most powerful experiences of my life to date. It's been both painful and cathartic, both a difficult reminder and a fulfilling release. It's given me an opportunity to revisit those areas of my life that for many years dictated how I felt about who I was. For as far back as I can remember there have been many people who have greatly influenced and shaped my life; there were those who helped to redirect me in order to find out just what it was that I had been so reluctant to face up to for so long. If you are one of those rarities, and only you will know who you are, I thank you.

My life has changed so colossally in the past couple of years. I would just like to mention a few people who have been close to me since I started out on this journey, who have witnessed the good times and the bad times, and also the individuals who steered me while I wrote this book.

Carole Blake, my agent and close friend, who has been a rock of support and encouragement through the tough times. Marian Finucane, Ireland's most endearing broadcaster. Marian's empathetic style has made her unique in her profession. It was following my interview with Marian on her radio show that this book finally received the momentum it needed to be completed. Anne Farrell and Tara Campbell, producers of *The Marian Finucane Show*. They persuaded me to 'speak out' that morning about depression. We lifted the lid that day and it hasn't gone back on the pot since then, nor I believe will it ever again.

My own producer and great friend Maggie Stapleton, an intuitive and wonderful woman who says it like it is.

My amazing team of publishers at Hodder Mobius. Both in London, to Rowena Webb and Esther Jagger for a class job of editing this book: they have added much extra magic and greater empathy; to Sheila Crowley, who was travelling from Dublin airport into the city on the morning of that fateful interview. Sheila called me within ten minutes of it finishing and asked me to write the book and tell my story. I call that Providence, Sheila – thank you; to Nyree Jagger and her publicity team; and to all at Hodder Headline Ireland: Breda Purdue and Ella Shanahan and their team for doing such a fine job 'at home'.

Eileen and Joe, my parents; Dave and Amy, my brother and sister; I love you dearly.

Finally, my strongest heartfelt gratitude goes to my family: to Jacqui; and to my three daughters, Kerri, Katie and Aibhin. Without you this journey of self-discovery, which at times felt like a fight for survival, might not have made as much sense as it does now, looking back, knowing you were there for me, and knowing how much you love me. I can only hope you know just how much I love you too.

In 1999 I was diagnosed with clinical depression. For years before then I had been living a life I despised, a life that always felt beyond my control. It affected my job, tore into my family relationships and took me to the brink of suicide. Yet today I am fit and healthy, happier than I have been in many years, successful, independent, ambitious, and more hopeful and optimistic about the future than I could have ever imagined. There is no sign in any aspect of my life of the depression that almost destroyed me.

These days I eat and sleep well. I enjoy my work, presenting a daily high-profile radio show on RTE 2FM, the national network in Ireland, and in my spare time I write bestselling novels. I exercise every day – or as often as I can, allowing for other commitments. Even on the days I don't exercise, I look forward to the next day when I can. This continues to send the right messages to my immune system, telling it I am continuing to feel better every day. I am spiritually well grounded and have a life that, years ago, I could not have imagined feeling fulfilled by. There are the usual daily problems and headaches, of course, but now I can face them and overcome them. Depression no longer exists in my life. Instead of being a slave to it, I have turned it into something that works for me.

I don't actually like the word 'depression', either as a clinical diagnosis or in its many broader uses. But I shall continue to use it throughout this book because, after all, it is a word that most people can instantly relate to – even if it tells them little, if anything, about a condition that encompasses a far greater range of emotions, complications and misery than simply a single state of mind. I prefer to think of this condition as the 'Stuck Syndrome'. 'Stuck' is a word that sums up the way I felt for years. 'Depression' told me nothing about my life, explained even less to me whenever I tried to rationalize it; it made more sense to me to describe the way I felt as 'being stuck'. It was as if I had been ill-made for life's demands, as if I had been shunted off down some overgrown, neglected siding at the back of a station where the trains no longer stopped. I felt I had been deserted by something inside me, that I had been left looking in on the lives of people I had once belonged to, whether I was in company, in conversation, or in love.

While depression is not fatal in itself, it makes living a normal, happy, useful life impossible and can lead to suicide. Suicide is on the increase, perhaps most worryingly among young people. Either we are not hearing the message or we prefer to look the other way. I believe it is the former, and health care professionals need to find a way of speaking louder and in a language that people don't find threatening. Within the next fifteen years, depression will outstrip cancer and AIDS worldwide as a cause of chronic ill health. We can no longer afford to turn a blind eye to depression, packing it away neatly in the loft like the Christmas decorations once the season has passed. My understanding of this bizarre disorder, and the ways in which I was able to vanquish it, have made me what I am today – remoulded and refined me into what I am happy with: being just me.

This book is about a way of living and a method of tapping into the intuitive strength that we all possess, and making it strong enough to empower us to overcome our darkest hours and put them behind us for good. It's a story of survival, a quest for improvement and a journey beyond the stifling effects and the stigma of this emotional crisis that used to beset my life. It's about making sense of something that seems so senseless; it's about taking back control, cultivating confidence and self-esteem; it's about how I got my life in order so that happiness and hope could be restored to me as quickly as possible, and I could get on with the business of enjoying my life. And after qualifying as a psychotherapist and counsellor I have worked with numerous other sufferers from depression, helping them to discover the causes of their acute misery and confusion and to develop a life that has led many of them beyond this stifling, stagnating condition.

Above all, this is a book of hope, gathered from my own experience, my studying, research and writing, and from talking to and learning from those who suffer from depression and have been both generous and forthcoming with their time and their personal experiences. If we don't have hope we are in serious trouble. Unfortunately it seems to be an increasingly rare commodity in this age of material affluence, social fragmentation and personal aspiration – all of which have led, sadly, to the isolation of the individual.

Since coming to understand my own depression, and moving beyond it, I have studied a number of areas of psychology relating to the reasons why people get depressed. Despite what many medical professionals may tell you, there *are* straightforward answers to many of the questions you have perhaps been asking for a long time. I hope you will find some of those answers here.

I don't claim to know all the answers, of course, but through the years I have discovered quite a few. What you will find between the covers of this book is the story of a journey: impressions, feelings, reasons and explanations – all extremely personal, all of them my own. You won't find a bundle of scientific facts, and I have aimed as far as possible to avoid medical jargon and technical terms.

It was never my intention to set out to disprove the medical theories of depression, even though I can't help frowning at some of them. I do believe, however, that the field of psychiatry in the ongoing search for ways to help sufferers of depression, needs to sit up and take note of what is really going on in the world today. It needs to develop a more embracing, sympathetic attitude to the individual who might be in a state of suffering that he or she is incapable of either understanding or explaining. There are some fascinating scientific theories about what causes depression, but, despite the research that claims to be finding out more and more about this mysterious condition, the recovery rate among people who rely solely on psychiatric help is not that good. I made a full recovery from depression, but I had to do most of the groundwork on my own – and that is also what this book is about.

Beyond the first stage of recovery lies a voyage of discovery, at times emotionally charged, at times difficult and painful, but always hugely rewarding and satisfying provided you hide nothing from yourself and allow it to unfold. If you take honesty as your guide, this journey will change your life and give you more hope and motivation than you could ever imagine. It changed mine. This is my story.

1

DARKNESS IN THE AFTERNOON

I remember it all so clearly now. I wanted to kill myself that afternoon, not for any specific reason other than that now the pain refused to go away. I lay perfectly still on the sweat-soaked bedsheet and listened for sounds, voices, laughter, music from the kitchen radio, my daughters singing or their innocent quarrelling – any recognizable noise that might help me find my bearings in this intolerable silence. My mouth and skin seemed desert-dry. I felt like I had a very high fever, but I knew nothing would show up on the thermometer – just like the previous day, and the day before that. For months now it had been like this, and getting worse all the time.

Bright sunshine crept through a slit in the curtain, its glare catching the side of my face each time the curtain lifted. Even though my eyes were closed, the sunshine hurt. I tried to figure out how long I had been sleeping the sleep of the dead. Why was it that I could sleep so soundly and wilfully in the daytime, when the rest of the world carried on about its business without a care, yet I could rarely sleep at night? The house sounded empty, hollow and lifeless, like it always felt when I woke in the late afternoon. The clock said 4.45.

I wanted it to be early morning. That way, I could avoid the blackest part of my day: the evenings, when the fading light brought an unbearable detachment that had caused me to shut out everyone and everything that I held dear. Closing my eyes in silence in the afternoon was like I imagined putting a sick dog out of its misery would be. The evenings brought with them the smell of food and the clatter of cutlery and plates and pots and dishes, but I had no appetite. It brought school homework and the gentle request from one or other of the girls, 'Dad, will you help me with this, please?' And while I would summon up some strength and attempt to make sense of modern mathematics, she might ask in an even softer tone, 'Dad, what's wrong with you? Are you all right?' And I might smile, and say, 'Of course I'm all right, darling, I'm just tired. I was up very early this morning.' And she might appear content and relieved by my excuse, but that was all it was. Because inside I was dying. My life was dissolving, and I felt there was nothing I could do to slow down the pace of decay.

Then again, I was hoping it wasn't early morning. That would have meant having to get up and face another day, having to entertain three hundred thousand people on Ireland's favourite breakfast radio show. I was responsible for getting all these listeners out of bed, showered, fed and on their way to school and work on time, with regular time checks, news bites, chunks of useful information, witty comments and items from the morning news. I was their Mr Zany, as one tabloid called me: 'Funny . . . witty . . . wry . . . Mr Zany . . . eclectic . . . pithy . . . engaging.' As I lay there on the crumpled sheet I tried to imagine myself as this character. Was this really me? And I begged something inside to give me a little bit of extra strength to get up, but there wasn't anyone listening. I wondered if I could talk to somebody about what was happening to me, but then I wondered exactly what was happening to me. I could hardly turn to a friend and ask for advice when I wasn't sure what was going on in the first place.

'It's like this. I go to bed and spend the day there, and then I get up and watch television for a while and go back to bed. I feel like shit!'

I imagined him thinking, *He's just bone-lazy. Too much time to kill.* Then he'd say, 'No wonder you feel like shit! Get up off your ass and pull yourself together. Get a life and stop feeling sorry for yourself. Go out for a long walk and enjoy this beautiful weather. Think of all the people who aren't as lucky as you are – they'd give their right arm to be doing your job.' And then I imagined him thinking, *He's winding me up. He's in such good form every morning I have to switch him off to catch my breath!*

And so I didn't ask for anything, other than to die.

I looked out on to the landing and imagined slinging my leather trouser belt around the banisters that led to the attic, placing a noose around my neck and gently easing myself off the top stair. I wondered how long it would take before I could no longer feel the pain of suffocation and what the moment of death might be like . . . a release, a relief. Tears streamed down my cheeks on to the pillow as I tried to push the thoughts out of my head, but there was little to replace them. I couldn't believe that I was lying here contemplating taking my own life, when only hours before I had been sitting in front of a microphone and telling thousands of people that it was a beautiful day.

'Morning, everyone . . . it's great to be alive.' Jesus, how could I sound so convincing and yet wish for the complete opposite?

Was this the start of some disease such as cancer or a brain tumour? Why had I been getting bad headaches for no apparent reason? Was this how terminal illness manifested itself in the early stages? My mind was tortured to the point where I wanted to rip out my brain and feel nothing. Much of the time I did feel nothing – a strange irony of depression, I found out later. I had once begged God to stop this and to help me, but by now I had suspended belief that such a benevolent ear was listening. No one was listening. No one understood this, not even me.

Downstairs a phone was ringing. I could have reached out and answered the call on the bedroom extension, but I didn't. I had switched its ringer off, because the slightest hint of noise would frequently make me fly into a rage now. The distant ringing wasn't as jarring and distracting as it would have been close by me. Eventually the caller rang off. And as I closed my eyes, the pain stopped again.

I went down to the kitchen, bare-footed and cold. Jacqui was sitting behind the kitchen door, where she always sat while she prepared the evening meal. She didn't look away and I could see her puffy red eyes, and the tears streaming down her cheeks on to the table. She hadn't bothered to answer the phone either. I pretended not to notice that she had been crying, in the hope that we wouldn't have to talk about this rotten, fucked up life that I had handed to her – a life that had turned her into a prisoner. Her whole existence seemed to revolve around my unpredictable state. It was as though her life had become filled with restrictions, as if she needed permission to exist behind the lifeless constraints that my behaviour had placed on her effervescent personality. Even in my confused state, I could see she was no longer the woman I used to know. She seemed to be dying with me, but I didn't know what I should do to stop feeling this way.

As I reached for the kettle, she said it. 'You need help. We can't go on like this.'

They were the words I never wanted to hear. They stank of the truth, but I didn't want them coming from her. 'We can't go on like this' reeked of selfishness to me, as if she was sick of caring for someone who was sick. I didn't want to admit I was sick, but I wanted her to believe silently that I was and to understand. Understand what? Maybe that might take the onus off me understanding it – maybe then I might not have to be the one to go looking for the awful bloody elusive answer. If I didn't say it out loud, then no one had to know the seriousness of the problem; but she knew. It was just the way she chose to say it that made me feel hurt and angry – but then again, everything did at that stage. I was a loaded weapon full of hurt and anger.

'What do you mean, *we* can't go on like this?' I snapped back defensively, trying to show her that she was blowing things out of all proportion. 'Just let me get through this. It's not as serious as you make it out to be,' I added, probably more resentfully than I had intended.

Then she started to cry again. This was a situation I had never been good at handling. There was no point in talking rationally if she was going to cry her way through what I had to say. Ironic that I still thought I was behaving and speaking rationally.

'I can't live like this any more,' she sobbed. 'I want my life back the way it used to be. I want to be happy again. I want *you* to be happy. I want to be able to come home knowing that you'll be in good form, that you won't be dug into that arm-chair in the corner, that you'll look forward to helping the girls with their homework, that we can go places as a couple, as a family, out for meals and the pictures, instead of tiptoeing around the house in case we wake you, or in case you explode and start ranting about how inconsiderate I am and that I don't understand you or how you feel any more. *I have feelings too!*' She stood up, pushed the table back and ran out of the kitchen.

I leaned against the drainer and folded my arms tightly as if to prevent myself falling apart. The self-loathing I felt – a feeling I still recall more than any other sensation or memory from that awful period of my life – was overpowering. I hated myself so much that I grabbed a clump of hair on top of my head and pulled it until I could hear the roots snapping. At that moment I hated everything I was. I could have reached out and grabbed the bread knife and cut my throat, I despised myself so much.

Self-loathing turned to anger. *How dare she say such hurtful things if she knows I need help!* I thought over and over. Why couldn't she try to understand that this wasn't my fault, that whatever was rotting my mind and my life was beyond my control, that I needed her to show patience and understanding? 'For better for worse . . . in sickness and in health . . .' Had she forgotten the afternoon twelve years ago when she made that promise? Why did she always want everything *her* way?

The anger was distorting every single thought that surfaced. I was furious with what I had become and whatever it was that was making me feel this way, bitter that my wife – the one person to whom I had looked for support – seemed to want to wash her hands of me, indignant that she thought I needed professional help, and resentful because she was insinuating that I was no longer a good father.

It was easier to shift the blame on to my nearest and dearest – easier than to own up to the truth, and what that truth might entail. *If we leave this alone for long enough*, I thought, *it might just go away as mysteriously as it came.*

It didn't of course. The black afternoons and blaming and bitter recriminations continued until eventually I saw a doctor – though even that was more by chance than intention – who presented me with the truth about what I had guessed, yet denied to myself, all along. Yet the mere mention of that word 'depression' created such a sense of fear in me, that it might as well have been a prison sentence.

Despite the small glimmer of hope my doctor helped me to feel that morning as he told me I was going to be all right, all I could think of for many weeks afterwards was that this monster called depression was inside me, lurking somewhere in the dark places that I knew were there but wasn't too inclined to face. Yes, I was unwell; but where was I unwell, and what did I ever do that caused me to get this 'sickness' that was making me want to kill myself?

2

THE SEEDS OF DEPRESSION

People often say schooldays are meant to be the happiest days of your life. Not in my case they weren't. I was a tall, gangly kid with no self-esteem and totally lacking in self-confidence. From the start I felt different, knew I wasn't like the others. There were days I wished I could be like them, brave and loud and carefree, but I couldn't. I hated games and any form of physical contact, and always managed to bunk off sports. In class I hated raising my hand, equally hated being picked on by a teacher to answer a question or comment on a topic. Right through school, from the time I was six years old, I was bullied by other children.

We were taught by members of an Irish religious order, the Christian Brothers, in a typical setting where discipline was exerted through corporal punishment. A short, bulky, stiffened leather strap with coins inserted between the layers to give it greater impact was the preferred method of punishment. For variety, boots and fists were occasionally used. I never felt the wrath and the beatings that these strong grown men dealt out to small boys were deserved, let alone appropriate.

I was eleven when I was sexually abused by a member of another religious order. It took place first on a scout holiday at a college and retreat centre in the Irish midlands and continued on and off for almost a year while my abuser became friendly with my parents and visited my house. Although he never did anything to me under their roof, he persuaded them on a number of occasions to let me travel back to the college, where he committed acts of indecency on me in his bedroom under a picture of the Sacred Heart. I desperately wanted to tell my parents what was happening, but he swore I would live to regret it if anyone found out. So they went on thinking he was kind and trustworthy, and that the trips to the country during the long school holidays were good for me.

I still recall those train journeys back to the college, alone and petrified as each stop brought me a station closer to this monster. There I sat, wondering what he must have been thinking as he waited on the platform for my train to arrive, wondering what he was going to do to me and how I could avoid him touching me. I never succeeded.

When I was a child, the Catholic Church dictated most of what we did and how we lived – adults as well as children. I was always taught that its teachings must be adhered to, that its values were indisputable and infall-ible, that its priests and brothers and nuns were faultless in their striving for spiritual perfection. Its power and control were unquestionable.

Yet behind this imposing façade lay something rotten, which would eventually destroy the Church as we knew it: sexual abuse against young boys and girls. Apart from my own experience, I had heard rumours that two boys in my class had had their trousers pulled down and their genitals fondled by one of the Christian Brothers who taught us. But no child dared to acknowledge in those days that he or she had been molested by a man so holy and so 'without sin' in the eyes of our parents and grandparents and peers. To do so would have led to accusations of being the devil's child, as I was told one afternoon many years later by a priest when I was nineteen and I felt the whole abuse period needed to be brought into the light and seen for what it really was: a sin against my young innocence.

During the preceding years I had been putting down layer upon layer of anxiety and fear, which was fuelling the existing mix of low self-esteem, indecisiveness and self-loathing. I believed I was ugly, stupid, crass and worthless, that I had nothing to offer to the world that a school system and my parents' love and concern seemed to be preparing me for.

Then, after that dreadful childhood experience, I made a pact that I would never trust anyone again. I had always taken a shine to people who were nice to me, but this man, who had picked me out from the rest of my scout troop, who had put me on a pedestal and shown me great respect, who had given me every good and honourable reason to entrust him with a love that I had previously only felt for my mother and father, who had bought me gifts and made me feel good and strong about myself, changed something. The 'nice person' I had first seen turned out to be an evil predator. He hurt me irrevocably, dropped me like a carton of eggs, smashing every single one.

I began to check locks and lights compulsively, listening to the voice in my head that constantly reminded me that I needed to do so, coming down to the kitchen in the middle of the night to press door handles for the umpteenth time in case something awful should happen to my family if I failed in my self-appointed task. It became so bad that I developed a ritual of checking a handle or lock by touching it seven times, then four, then two, then one. If anything upset this routine, even the remotest thought flashing across my mind, it would have to be done all over again. I could not stop worrying about disaster and disease, and washed my hands constantly until they turned red and raw. The condition, I learned later, is called Obsessive Compulsive Disorder or OCD, and is closely related to some forms of depression.

I can recall thinking at the age of twelve that I was mad, and that it was only a matter of time before I would have to be committed to St Brendan's, the local psychiatric hospital with its huge grey walls and massive iron gates. I lived in fear of the place, having heard exaggerated stories about its inmates who supposedly lived out their lives wandering along dimly lit corridors, shuffling about in slippers and dressing gowns free of any sharp items and belts that might give them ideas. I never knew how I might finally 'blow', but I always remember thinking that I wanted my mother to be close by if it ever happened. I guess I knew she would be the only one who would understand, and explain to the men in white coats when they arrived to take me away.

As a teenager, I wasn't very expressive. There seemed to be a constant rawness about life. I never felt relaxed in the company of people I didn't know, never felt comfortable being asked for my opinion. I thought a great deal, but they were mostly negative thoughts. I even thought about all the hard thinking – ruminating – I was doing; but I never felt much like talking or discussing things or joining in the easiest conversations. Ruminating, literally, means chewing the cud – it's what cows do when they regurgitate the grass they've eaten earlier and chew it all over again. And that's precisely what I did in my mind, constantly going over the same thoughts over and over again so that I never got anywhere. My low self-esteem was even affecting the way I dealt with my thoughts and perceptions based on what was happening around me.

I believe that our self-esteem comes as part of a package – that it is inherent in our make-up and part of the blueprint which creates us and which we carry into the world with us when we are born. Just as with curly hair and long noses and other physical traits and similarities that we inherit from our parents and grandparents, we are also infused with a hybrid selection of their personality traits. Shaped and moulded through hundreds of generations over thousands of years, later in our development they will manifest themselves as moods and emotions to give us what we call our true feelings.

My father was self-employed, a very hard-working man who travelled a lot on business and was therefore away a lot when my brother and sister and I were children. I was amazed that he still had enough energy to take us on our bikes to the park at weekends. My family life, in fact, contained all the ingredients for a flawless childhood and we were a very happy family. My parents couldn't have cared for us better and always put us first in any decisions they made, and I would never dream of faulting my parents or my brother and sister for anything that wasn't right in my childhood. I was the one who was ill made for the tough demands of living, short on the skills that most people take for granted, low on the personality characteristics needed in order to sail through life's constantly changing currents.

I remember spending lots of time with my mother, time I used to look forward to greatly because her power to reassure me remained unsurpassed until I met my wife. Although, like my father, my mother was strong-willed, she was more mellow and reserved and gentler in her character. She was always a softly spoken woman, a great listener who could take away mental pain with a simple smile or a gentle touch of the hand.

'Mam, why do people go mad?' I asked her one evening as I finished my homework and she was doing the ironing. I was thirteen at the time and sorely tormented by my obsessive routines.

She seemed to compose herself, like she did when she was going to say something serious, and studied my pained expression. 'Why do you ask?'

'I think I'm going mad, and I'm really scared,' I replied, trying hard not to panic and avoiding eye contact.

'You're not going mad,' she said as she sat opposite me at the kitchen table, close enough to touch my hand. 'You're just trying to deal with feelings that are a bit confusing and upsetting right now. There are loads of changes going on both inside and outside. We've all felt like this.'

I wanted to tell her that she could never have felt like I felt at that moment.

'Try not to let them upset you so much,' she went on, 'and talk to me, and keep talking to me, and we'll work through it together. I promise, nothing is too bad to tell me. Nothing!'

In the space of a few minutes, her words and her love had put my life back on track. Then one afternoon I told my mother about the sexual abuse, and once I started I couldn't stop. She urged me to keep talking, to keep telling. My stomach was in a knot and the tears felt like they would never stop falling. It was the first time I had ever seen my mother cry, too. She held me and stroked my hand and just let me rock backwards and forwards with the pain I was releasing after years of locking it away too deeply inside.

Mothers are intuitive. Later she told me she had regularly noticed my strange behaviour and suspected that something might have been wrong. She had wanted to confront me but chose not to, waiting for an appropriate moment. I just happened to get there before her.

Soon afterwards the OCD symptoms started to die away. The relief that came with my revelation was as palpable as if someone had just burst a balloon with a sharp pin and taken away the pressure. Within weeks I found my mind had settled somewhat and the rituals and terrifying thoughts finally left me. I started to receive counselling and decided, with the help of my parents, not to go to the police.

However, the damage had been done. According to sociologist Morris Massey, what he calls the Modelling Period in a child's life, between the ages of eight and thirteen, is the time when we begin to realize that we are not all the same, that we are quite different in many ways from others, including our own parents. It is the time when we choose heroes and mentors and make their values and beliefs our own. Massey believes that our values – the mental measuring stick we use to determine what is and is not important throughout our lives – are based on our experiences when we were ten or eleven years old. This, of course, was exactly the period in my own life when I was sexually abused. And so, despite having shared my terrible secret, I believe depression had already taken hold of me, feeding on the lack of confidence and self-esteem that had always been there.

3

THE CREATIVE IMPULSE

Fortunately for me, I found two means of escape from the unhappiness I felt during my childhood. First, I pushed the bleaker aspects of my schooldays aside by burying my head in my books in preparation for the new life which I knew existed beyond those 'prison walls'. I loved English lessons, read as much as I could of the great writers and tried to be as creative as I could in my essay writing. I was also lucky to have a wonderful English teacher, Luke Brady, who I'm glad to say is still a great friend. Later, this love of language would develop into another safety valve, writing novels.

Secondly, from a very early age, perhaps as young as six, beautiful music had become a place for me to hide. The gentler songs of the late sixties and early seventies, with their messages of reassurance and confirmation, helped me to realize feelings that I couldn't otherwise have identified. The way these gifted singers and song-writers expressed themselves helped to lighten the torment I seemed to drag around after me like other kids dragged their wooden carts and home-made trolleys behind them. Music gave me an opportunity to reach out and find some meaning in the strange, painful con-fusion that permanently dogged me. The songwriters' ability to describe such pained feelings so beautifully gave me some sort of inner strength and resilience. I remember wondering if they knew how important their personal stories and poignant feelings really were – spelling out, as they did, something that touched my own situation so perfectly. These were songs for people who felt so lost and bruised that they were afraid to go looking for help.

We had an old record player at home, and I remember the first vinyl 45 my father bought me back in 1974. It was called 'Every Day', by Birmingham band Slade. I played it over and over until I had the words by heart, and knew instinctively there and then, at the age of thirteen, that some day I would be playing that song on the radio. Another which I listened to continually, having taped it from the radio when I was nine, was 'The Long and Winding Road'. There was no introduction – just the searching, scorching sound of Paul McCartney's voice. To this day it never ceases to take my breath away.

Such songs reached into me deeply, to a place that normally seemed impossible to touch. They released some of the pain that alone I was never able to fathom, never mind understand. I hummed them whenever I felt the emptiness that caused me to ask myself what I had ever done to deserve this, and why I felt so inadequate and so different from other kids and from my brother and sister. James Taylor, Harry Chapin and Gordon Lightfoot all sang about things that seemed relevant to my life. Perhaps the lyrics told the stories I wasn't able to express myself. I kept the volume turned up to keep the rest of the world at a distance.

Although the sentiments expressed in these songs were

sad, they served to soften this strange sense of absence I had nearly always felt, as if I had been left without an important engine part. As a result I had always felt I had no choice but to hold back, not to participate in whatever everyone else my age was perfectly keen and happy to get involved in. From an early age I had often felt as if my head would explode, as if something was going on inside me that I had absolutely no control over – I had no knowledge of what it was, where it had come from, or why it always seemed to be there. All I know is that the music switched it off for a while, keeping it at bay like a trip switch protecting my senses and my sanity.

When I was fifteen, I realized what I wanted to do when I left school. I wanted a job where I could surround myself with this empowering music. It made me feel secure for some reason, made me feel wanted: there were times when I felt I could walk on its strength and felt energized by its sheer magnificence. These painful lyrics and exquisite guitar riffs made the hair on the back of my neck stand up and helped me to recognize that I was not alone, not different, not unique. While my friends created havoc on the dance floor of our school disco to Thin Lizzy and the Sex Pistols, I was more interested in listening to Arlo Guthrie singing about New Orleans. Or I would sit in my bedroom with my portable cassette player and a Gilbert O'Sullivan tape; inevitably, my favourite from that collection was called 'Alone Again Naturally'.

By the time I turned sixteen I wanted to be on the radio. Whenever I had the chance I would disappear into the make-believe world of my own radio show, sketching designs for the perfect studio, dreaming about the day I would sit in front of a microphone and generate the same kind of enthusiasm in my audience as I was feeling at that moment. Often, during lessons I didn't like, I made lists of songs I would play on my first broadcast. It was pure escapism, the one and only occasion in the day when I didn't feel on the outside, detached from conversation, a couple of inches too small to see over the windowsill of a normal life that everyone else had successfully scaled.

I left school in 1978 with respectable exam results and got my first 'proper' job, selling household linens in a department store in Dublin. I hated it, but it gave me a certain freedom that I had never experienced before. Within months I had moved to become a pensions accounts executive with a leading life assurance company in the city. Once again it was a depressing way of earning a living. I drifted along as my colleagues and I (without much interest on my part) applied ourselves to study programmes that would help us climb the ladder to promotion and greater responsibility. I really don't know how I would have coped if my dream job had not appeared on the horizon.

During my lunch breaks from the insurance office I always visited a small, run-down record shop around the corner, and the man behind the counter eventually came to know my taste in music. 'What would you like to hear, Gar?' he would ask when he spotted me thumbing through the old LP sleeves in the bargain bins. I was into soulful music: anything with lots of orchestral strings and harmony vocals and sad lyrics and wistful chorus lines. The Sound of Philadelphia and Tamla

Motown put my spirit into orbit. In the late 1970s pirate radio was flourishing in Dublin, and one afternoon, when we had been chatting away for such a long time that I was going to be late returning to work, he said he was in a position to offer me a job on the biggest and most popular of them, Radio Dublin. If he had given me a choice between that and winning the big prize on the National Lottery, I think I would have plumped for the radio.

Radio, and particularly my slot on a Saturday evening, became everything to me. Nothing else mattered outside those two hours speaking to faceless strangers and friendly voices and lonely hearts. At eighteen I had become a local hero. I changed my name to Tony Gareth because I thought it sounded cool. Most people I worked with in those days on pirate radio had changed their names. We were outlaws, thumbing our noses at the authorities who called people like us, who flouted the law and broadcast illegally, criminals. And if we were out-laws we had to have catchy, roguish names that would roll off the tongue and catch listeners' imaginations.

I quickly advanced to secure my own week-night radio slot, while neglecting the day job – I quit any notion I had had of becoming an accountant, dropped my study schedule, ran up a huge flexitime overdraft and basically just paid lip service to the people who were paying my wages.

'It's sad, Gareth, but we had great plans for you in here,' one of the men in suits said to me one morning. 'It's a pity you've chosen to throw away such a golden opportunity.'

I hadn't. In fact I had just realized my true ambition in life. The outer personality was taking hold fast, redirecting everything I had been considering up to that point. The front man on the radio would eventually take over my entire life and dictate almost everything that would happen to me for some twenty years to come.

4

VOCATIONS RIGHT AND WRONG

In 1981 I announced proudly to my family and friends that I was planning to study for the priesthood. This might seem an extraordinary departure given that I had never mentioned the thought to anyone before, and considering the bullying and abuse to which I had been subjected by some of Ireland's religious. But, as I have said, the influence of the Church was powerful in Ireland, and the idea of this way of life had in fact been sitting quietly at the back of my mind for years, gently chipping away, making me more interested and more curious about its attractions and rewards.

I wanted to be a priest who lived in a parish among my people, serving their needs and helping them in every way that I could. If this sounds like the 'typical' vocation, then that's what it was. I believe it was typical of what most young men in the past felt when they entered college to study for the priesthood, and I think I must have managed to dissociate my boyhood maltreatment from the positive aspects of the priesthood.

The men who had abused and bullied me were, of course, not priests but religious brothers, and therefore different. The priests I knew at that point in my life were good, wholesome men (although later I would discover through shocking headlines in the media that a small minority of their kind were anything but good and wholesome). The priests I knew were the sort of men who were appalled by the horrific revelations of child abuse that began to emerge in the early 1980s.

At any rate, for some years I had been impressed by a number of men whose commitment to their vocation left me in no doubt that there was tremendous satisfaction and happiness to be had from helping other people in such a capacity. They seemed content, yet always willing to reach out. They were 'on call', so to speak, for anyone in trouble – people-helpers of the greatest and at the same time humblest of calibres. I liked this notion of devoting the remainder of my life to such a calling.

One priest in particular who influenced me was a Marist called Vincent Duffy, a Dundalk man who had entered theological college in his mid-forties after enjoying what he called a 'wild life'. 'A late vocation', as he referred to himself, he was a wonderfully happy, charming and loving individual who always put others first. He gave me the impression that there could be no life more fulfilling than that of a priest in the service of God.

Vincent came to my home parish as a curate in the late seventies, and I got to know him through his association with the local youth club. I was much taken by his wisdom and his worldly experience: he had dated women, and I liked that idea. It made him a 'real' man, not callow and naïve and inexperienced like so many priests I had met through the years. This man spoke my language and offered hands-on advice, and we became great friends.

The attraction of the priesthood overshadowed everything now, including my intended radio career, even though I didn't think there would be a problem doing some part-time radio work while I was studying. I suppose in hindsight it gave me an opportunity to get out of a day job I hated into something that held great appeal because it was so different from anything I had ever contemplated before. So in September that year I left home and entered Clonliffe seminary in Dublin. But by eleven o'clock that first night I knew I had made the biggest mistake of my life.

I lay in bed in a small, bare box of a room, wondering what on earth I had done, envisaging what lay ahead, and poring over all the things in my life I had just deliberately said goodbye to for ever: freedom, a career with music, marriage, companionship with other women on a level that would be frowned upon by my superiors. I felt nauseous that night, and for a long time afterwards, but decided nevertheless to stay for a year. After all, I had quit my insurance job, received many expensive presents from relatives and friends and had the going-away party of all parties. My parents, delighted at the prospect of a priest in the family, had also made a generous donation to the college to cover my education for the remainder of the year, so I decided if for no other reason to stay in order to honour the commitment they had shown to me.

That night a form of depression returned that I had not experienced for many years, not since I had lain awake in bed as a teenager battling with the demons that the memory of the sexual abuse randomly threw at me. The terror that consumed my thoughts right through those hours of darkness convinced me I shouldn't be there. The more I contemplated that notion, the more I realized that my whole existence up to that point seemed to consist of having been in the wrong place at the wrong time.

Why had I chosen the priesthood? I searched hard for positive, convincing answers that might persuade me I was simply feeling a little homesick, but it ran much deeper. All the aspects of my life that I had neatly swept under the carpet for years were resurfacing now, like a crowd that had been queuing for the best bargains on the first morning of a shop sale; the door was thrown open, they surged into the store and my mind seemed to lose its grip on what it had been holding back all these years. I lay there helplessly battling the most frightening thoughts and memories, many of which I had clean forgotten about. They danced around my bed in the pitch darkness as I tried to distract myself by listening to the eager voices of people passing up and down the corridor outside my door, and to the sounds of late night traffic and the sirens of emergency vehicles beyond the high walls of the college.

At one point I wanted to throw up, but the bathroom seemed too far away. I got up and walked around the dark room, reluctant to turn on the light in case someone walking down the corridor should knock on the door and introduce himself. I wanted to ring Vincent Duffy, who was now my spiritual adviser, and beg him to come and fetch me. But I knew I couldn't.

Why was I here? I had thrown everything away: my job, which I hated but which right now represented an attractive alternative; my friends, who I believed would never treat me the same again; and my growing fondness for a young woman to whom I could in the future never be anything other than a good friend, and she to me.

I just hadn't given enough practical consideration to this giant step. Perhaps the romantic sense of being the great helper had clouded my logic, and only now was I starting to realize that the priesthood was not exactly what I had anticipated. I think I must have been idealizing it. Whatever, the image I had had in my mind was nothing ike the real thing. Here I was, locked up in a building full of men who had chosen never to become sexually involved with anyone for the rest of their lives. The voice in my head was telling me that such a decision was utterly ridiculous and intrinsically wrong. Human beings were made for closeness and companionship, to find mates whom we could spend the rest of our lives with, not to shut ourselves away from society and intimacy. For me, the expression 'men in black' holds no associations with a popular movie.

College life was, on the whole, uncomfortable. While my 'secular' friends in the world outside the seminary tumbled out of bed in the morning, busied themselves with their daily jobs and then went out in the evening with their girlfriends, I rose at seven, dressed in clerical garb – black cassock, white collar and shiny black shoes – and went to mass. While my mates were driving their cars into the city, I was singing hymns. From there we went to the refectory for breakfast, prepared by three dear nuns who treated me like an adopted son, and then on to college to study theology, philosophy and sociology. Once again I threw myself unequivocally into my books, studying as hard as I could on my own every night. It was my way of keeping the demons at bay. But I also made some good friends, who remain close to me today.

College life could also be dangerous. Here were two hundred young men locked up behind high walls with no outlet for the forbidden, unmentionable, dammed up testosterone. Practical jokes became the order of the day. One student was held upside down by his ankles from a fourth-floor window late one night for almost half an hour. This was definitely not funny, but our levels of pent-up energy were sky-high most of the time. We were urged to pray in order to distract our minds from 'matters of the flesh'.

After three months of college, quite certain by now that I had no real vocation for the priesthood, I realized I had fallen in love with the woman I would eventually marry. I had first met Jacqui on a bus when I was still working at the insurance office. I was hurrying home to change out of my business suit and head for the radio station for that evening's show; she was coming home from school. Jacqui lived close to my parents' house, so we knew each other by sight, and that evening she handed me a request to play for a friend of hers. Jacqui was extremely attractive and likeable – while making it quite clear that it was her friend, not she, who fancied me. In the months that followed we bumped into each other occasionally, stopping to chat.

We became closer, soulmates, once I made my decision to study for the priesthood. At first it was nothing more than a platonic friendship, although I had very strong feelings for her. We leaned heavily on each other for advice, opinions and friendship. It was perfectly normal for someone studying for the priesthood to find women attractive, I was told. However, as time went on my feelings grew a lot deeper. She was out of work and so we met regularly on my half-days off from college, often sitting over a coffee, occasionally taking in a film in a city cinema, but never anything more intimate. We just sat and chatted and whiled away the hours, enjoying each other's company. Neither of us ever mentioned fancying each other, but there was an unspoken bond between us that grew stronger and stronger as the months went by. It was her company, and the feeling of looking forward to meeting her on a Thursday afternoon, that I believe kept me sane at this time.

I often thought about running away with her. What if I left the college late one night and together we headed for the North Wall, where the ferry left for Liverpool? We could set up a new life together in the Yorkshire Dales or in Scotland – some place where no one would ever find us. The notion of running away appealed to me, when what I should have been doing was addressing my problems.

It was during my first summer holidays from college that we acknowledged to each other how we felt. The weekend before I was meant to be packing for the new college term in September 1982 I announced to my parents that I wasn't going back. They were surprised initially, but quickly accepted my decision and supported me. I explained to the dean of the college that the priesthood was not an option for me and that celibacy was a twisted, macabre way of life for anyone, man or woman, to have to endure in the name of Jesus Christ. He smiled and thanked me for my opinion. Vincent Duffy, my friend and spiritual adviser, heard of my decision without rebuke. The night I was supposed to be back sleeping in my small box room, I took Jacqui to the pictures and we held hands.

In this day and age, serving as a priest is by no means easy. In fairness it never was, but in the light of the recent appalling Church scandals involving sexual abuse, and the disgraceful way in which the Church's leaders have dealt with its own offenders, priests are now feeling their own pain and confusion as they wonder what people must think of them after being so badly let down by the very people they look up to. It would be improper and unjust to tar all these men with the same brush.

Entering the seminary had been a decision made for all the wrong reasons. I know now it was simply another means of getting away from the battle that was going on inside me, the demand for reconciliation between the individual I really was within and the driven persona I was allowing to take control of the future. Perhaps my decision to study for the priesthood was an unconscious effort to exorcize the spirit that had been forcing me for years into a situation that would demand reform of my life, redirection so that I could be content on the inside as well as on the outside. Maybe seminary life and the priesthood were a better representation of what that true inner person really was at that time in my life.

So I swapped college life and celibacy for a full-time job on radio and a wonderful relationship with a woman who for so long I had thought could never be more than a good friend. I admire the men who went the full distance in college, who were ordained into a lonely, often relentless life serving their ministry. I'm grateful to be able to count some of these men among my best friends, and honoured that they consider me similarly.

5

LIGHTNING CHANGES

I have always been drawn to the beauty and power of simplicity. I believe now that sticking to the simple things in life allows each of us to enjoy our achievements and to admire many aspects of the world around us that we often miss out on when we make our lives cluttered and complicated. I know now that the beautiful simplicity of the priesthood was one of its main attractions for me. The men I admired were drawn to what appeared to me a simple task – devoting the rest of their lives to God in the service of others. As I have since discovered, placing the cares and needs of others above our own weakens the hold of depression and enables hope and inner personal strength to replace feelings of unworthiness and helplessness.

Unfortunately, I always mistook simplicity for inadequacy. I was, and still am to a degree, a perfectionist – someone who can all too readily interpret simplicity as an excuse to be lazy and neglectful. The indecisiveness that accompanied my severe bouts of depression did battle with my perfectionist tendencies, and perhaps this was what almost drove me over the edge: one enemy was telling me I just didn't care about anything, while the other was telling me I was a useless slacker.

To be able to accept simplicity and use it to your

advantage is an art form that offers many rewards, as I have discovered in my own life. It renders depression manageable and maintains it at a safe distance. To keep things simple for me today means to indulge in the things that give me the greatest happiness and satisfaction, and in doing so to fill the void that houses uncertainty and anger, confusion and self-loathing. And one of those things that give me tremendous happiness and satisfaction has always been music, whether enjoyed in private or shared with thousands on the airwaves.

For as long as I can remember, as far back as my first communion when I was seven, I hated having my photo taken, hated speaking in public – just like I was always shy and silent at official functions I was invited to attend. And yet I absolutely loved being on the radio! Is this a contradiction? I don't think so. Radio for me has always been a very personal form of communication, a one-to-one relationship between two people who never see each other. Yet we quickly become intimate elements in each other's lives. When we meet for the first time, people tell me they feel as though they have known me for years.

I suppose the word 'bizarre' might adequately describe my job. I sit in a small room for three hours every day on my own, surrounded by a small panel of controls and computer screens, and speak into a microphone, making friendly conversation with people I can't see; and yet I'm often reminded of how much this 'solo flight' each day touches the lives of so many people who make it their business to listen.

I was drawn to radio because, like the singers and songwriters who knew there were people out there who would love their songs and stories, I had always wanted to believe there would be people who might enjoy listening to what I wanted to chat about and the music I had always wanted to play for them. It made perfect sense for someone like me who shunned the bright lights of fame and publicity to want to sit in a quiet, undisturbed studio and play the music that had defined my life to people who might have felt in some small way the feelings I had experienced, and in turn the uplift and hope I always felt when I heard these familiar songs and voices.

My life has never been short of variety and upheaval; lightning change, I have often called it. Some of these changes have brought happiness; others have merely served to throw me back into the black pit of depression. I lost my job in radio in Dublin in 1983, when the government redrafted the legislation so that it became unlawful to work for a pirate radio station. The stations themselves were closed down, often involving confrontations between police and government officials on the one side and on the other rebel staff who resisted to the end. Eventually I opted to travel to Britain, where local radio was flourishing and the likelihood of a permanent, legal job appealed to me.

But first, in the early spring of 1983, I was offered a job on a British pirate station, the legendary Radio Caroline which had first operated in the sixties. Its original founder had recently purchased an old 300-foot fishing trawler, renamed the *Ross Revenge*, which was being kitted out in Bilbao in northern Spain before its long journey to the English coast, five miles off Clacton in Essex. I was about to become a real pirate, equipped with all the fantastic stories I had heard about some of the legendary names of the early days, like Tony Blackburn and Kenny Everett, on the first Radio Caroline.

In reality, life on board the *Ross Revenge* was a nightmare. We were promised regular deliveries of food and fresh water; during the six weeks I spent on board I don't think we had a single one. We were reduced to a diet of sausage pie and banana and pineapple soufflé, thanks to the masterly culinary skills of chef and occasional DJ Tony Scott. Stormy weather was frequent. There wasn't much to do outside the two four-hour shifts I spent on air entertaining an audience of almost 4 million, so I usually poured myself a large brandy, climbed into my narrow bunk in the dark, windowless cabin I called home, and listened for hours on end to the North Sea lapping on the other side of my cabin wall. Yet another depressing job. For some reason it always seemed as if I purposely ran away *into* these hopeless situations. I couldn't figure out why I was doing it over and over again. Was I never going to be happy?

As soon as someone offered to rescue me I jumped ship. I was taken off late one night during a Force 9 gale, in an open-topped lifeboat captained by a drunken retired skipper. After several hours at sea we docked in the peaceful confines of Brightlingsea harbour, almost 50 miles from London, at five-thirty in the morning.

I returned to Dublin the following day, but within a week had been offered a job back in England on a radio station in the West Midlands. Over the next few years I seemed to be permanently on the move around England, with jobs in Leeds, Luton and London, where I studied journalism with the BBC. By 1987 I had had enough. I wanted to come home and stay home. I was worn out, thin as a lath and doing all the wrong things in life.

I felt as if I had been drifting for ever, floating about on a tide I had little control over, and there never seemed to be any direction or plan. It was as if I had been washed ashore half a dozen times, on each occasion setting sail clumsily again, only to find myself back at the start. I spent money crazily, always far beyond what I could afford. My parents baled me out with cheques and money orders, while my brother back in Ireland quietly worked away at a good job and needed no such handouts. I envied the wholesome, well-directed life he had carved out for himself. He appeared to have a plan. He studied hard and was rewarded with the promotions he deserved. Despite the fact that he was younger I looked up to him for his fortitude and sensibility, neither of which I possessed in any great quantity. He seemed rational and well organized where I was scatterbrained and unpredictable. He had an agenda. I didn't. He was clever. I was lucky.

All the time, throughout the vicissitudes of those five years in England, I had continued to battle with my double existence: the shy, confused inner being who wanted a careful and didactic approach to life, and the outer creature who didn't care, who craved attention even though I felt uncomfortable with it, who demanded to live for the now, to take reckless chances and behave completely unlike the individual I knew I should be but hated being. And all the time I continued to run further and further away from confronting the questions I refused to ask out loud.

It only became consciously obvious to me in my last couple of years in England just how much music had helped me to stay reasonably steady, behaving like a natural mood enhancer. Before, I had worried greatly about how it was possible to be on a high while presenting my radio show and within hours to sink to depths that left me fighting for breath. Perhaps, I thought, I might be suffering from Bipolar Disorder, or manic depression as it used to be known. This condition is characterized by particularly extreme emotional highs and lows: frightening, often tragic depths of depression eventually replace periods of elation and euphoria. Whatever, I knew that music enabled me to cope.

During my time in England I made many friends, but my relationship with Jacqui had virtually ceased to exist. She came over from Dublin to visit me on a couple of occasions while I was living in Coventry, but then we lost contact for almost two years. On the afternoon in late August 1987 when I returned to Ireland I took a major chance and visited a jeweller's where I bought an engagement ring. Apart from our being out of touch I knew things might be a little frosty as I had been seeing someone else in England. Nevertheless I arrived at her house about seven that evening and proposed. It was either a yes or a visit to the pawnshop the next day. Happily she accepted, and we were married the following May.

I had already told her about being sexually abused as a young boy. She was shocked, but in her own way understanding. I could see tears welling up in her eyes as I explained to her what had happened. But I don't believe she recognized the symptoms of my depression until much later. It's difficult to recognize something which we misinterpret as being part of a person's intrinsic make-up. I had accepted a long time ago that some people are naturally sad, and had concluded that maybe I was one of those people. Like me, Jacqui may have thought that this was simply the way I was, and that was how she accepted me.

6

EMOTIONAL BLACKMAIL

I am a home bird at heart, a natural-born candidate for bouts of homesickness, even on short stays away from the place and people I love. Now, in the latter half of the eighties, I was happy to be back in Ireland, newly married and, having spent almost ten years knocking on their doors, soon to work for RTE, the national broadcasting network. While I waited on the call from RTE, I worked for a number of stations and nightclubs.

Jacqui and I bought a small house on the outskirts of Dublin city, which was a good distance from friends and family. Consequently we spent a lot of time together on our own and what socializing we did tended to be done in the pub. We were both delighted when Jacqui quickly became pregnant, but it changed our social habits. During her pregnancy she found alcohol nauseating: as she began to drink less, my own intake was on the increase. I know now that it was exacerbated by the depression which was beginning to take hold of me, but at the time I put it down to the combined pressures of the imminent arrival of our first child, moving into a new house and getting the hang of my new, high-profile job. None of these events, traumatic even in normal circumstances, was without its additional problems.

First, Jacqui's pregnancy was rife with serious problems. She bled quite heavily from the fifth month, developed toxaemia towards the seventh, and was then confined to bed until the date she was due to give birth. The house, it turned out, had been thrown up by cowboy builders whom we had to take to court. And what was shortly to happen to me at work played a strong role in my slow spiral downwards.

Having been bullied at school when I was a child, I was now about to receive the same unwanted attention at the hands of an individual I was in regular contact with through work. Quite a lot of bullying goes on in the entertainment industry, and it's usually to do with ambition and ego not among the creative types but at management level. Most creative people are sensitive and easily offended. This, I hasten to add, is not a character weakness by any means. By their very natures they find it difficult to accept criticism, especially when it comes from a bully. Over a 25-year career span, I have seen people in my own line of work being threatened with the sack if they don't comply with some diktat from someone in a position of higher authority, simply because refusal to do so might put that person out of favour with his own boss. What most of these types don't realize is that their future depends (or should depend) on the 'man at the coalface': the person holding the microphone.

It once happened to me many years ago, five minutes before I was due to present a part-time radio show. My contract was due for renewal within a few days, and I was gutted. What was I to think? My mind did somersaults throughout the show. My heart pounded and raced, my hands shook, my palms sweated and I prayed like I had never prayed in my life. Up to that point I had been surviving on short-term contracts that were only renewable if your boss liked you on the due day. While it happened a long time ago, I remember it as if it were yesterday.

To me, the effects of bullying are as destructive and as devastating as those of sexual abuse. Bullying behaviour is like a silent cancer eating away at my very core: a mere look or word can easily send me into self-destruct mode. It gnaws away at my self-esteem and self-confidence, undermines my values and beliefs, and blurs my goals so that the future seems hopeless while the present becomes a stagnant living hell. I back off, not just from the immediacy of this never-ending nightmare but from life generally. The bully, like a giant black crow on my windowsill, dominates my every waking moment and dictates the pace of my sleepless nights. Sooner or later, I know, I am going to die under the weight of this dreadful ordeal, this silent abuser. I lose my appetite, lose weight, lose interest and eventually lose hope.

In the eyes of his mates, a bully is often regarded as a hero. The victim, on the other hand, may be perceived as a weakling who needs to learn how to stand up for himself. One thing is certain: bullying is a short cut to a severely depressed state of mind. The victim feels worth-less, like putty in the hands of someone or something far more powerful and influential. He or she is no longer in control – that role has been taken over by the bully. Having managed to tap into the very deepest level of his victim, the bully is now in the driving seat.

This former colleague knew how to manipulate me, as

he did so many others: to stab me and psychologically disembowel me without leaving the smallest physical trace. He used emotional blackmail and threats in the most cowardly way possible, since he believed he held the reins of my career. For the short time I worked with this individual I lived alone in a haunted house, aware that at any moment he could turn on me. Despite the pleasure my job as a radio presenter gave me on my good days, I gave serious consideration to emigrating to the USA. A friend of mine who was over there had offered me a daily radio show on one of Boston's most successful stations. A year later he moved to Chicago to be chief executive at that city's leading radio station, and repeated his offer. I was sorely tempted.

My moods, unsurprisingly, worsened and I found it increasingly difficult to sound happy and upbeat while on-air. This man's bullying, clever and covert, became a form of stalking. He followed me, phoned me and watched me, tracing almost every step I took from the moment I arrived at work each day. He listened to my show, dissected the comments I made, criticized my style, ridiculed my success and was constantly looking for ways to trip me up and further undermine my confidence.

Eventually I plucked up the courage to approach a superior. I tried to be tactful, afraid I might otherwise sound as if I was making excuses for not being up to the mark. But to my relief I was taken seriously and plans were made immediately to move the individual in question to another area of responsibility where we could have no further contact with each other. As luck would have it, I moved to a new broadcasting company shortly after this protracted torture ended.

The relief was palpable. In addition, after Jacqui's difficult pregnancy Kerri, the first of our three daughters, had been born perfectly healthy. And finally we managed to sell the problem house and moved to one closer to where we both came from, on the Navan Road on the north side of the city. We seemed to have left the bad times behind.

Sadly, it was an illusion. My depression was still lurking in the background, and it took even firmer hold of me later when a business investment which the two us had been interested in pursuing went pear-shaped, leaving us virtually penniless.

On a trip to London I had visited a franchise exhibition at Earls Court, where I had secured the rights to manufacture and sell personalized children's books on the Irish market. The idea was that we bought in the raw material from the UK and took orders for Christmas, christenings, birthdays and so on, printing the child's name into the storyline so that he or she became one of the characters in the book. It was a hugely exciting project, but we hadn't planned it properly or considered the possible pitfalls. The time was the early 1990s – a very bad time financially. Sterling was standing very high against the Irish punt, so we had to pay high prices for the books; their cost quickly outstripped the small profits we were making. At home, interest rates were soaring and it became hard enough to repay a mortgage, never mind trying to nurse a large overdraft and find outlets for our new business. The bank not only refused to extend our overdraft to help us keep trading, but called in the old one. We were, quite simply, broke.

I remember coming home from work one night in December and saying to Jacqui, 'It's all gone. I have thirty quid left in my pocket. Let's go and have a drink to celebrate Christmas!' Unfortunately, at this time the place of alcohol in my life was far greater than just an occasional ironic celebration.

7

DRINK: FRIEND AND FOE

During those dark days the drinking took me out of the black hole for a short while. It released the pain and enabled me to keep the present troubles and the future uncertainties at a small distance. Social drinking enabled me to take a break with friends who knew I was in trouble, but who preferred to keep me cheered and detached from all that, if only for the time I spent in their company. I was grateful to them. I felt that I deserved to drink – as much as I wanted to, when I wanted to. Life was a bitch, with contractual negotiations at work looking increasingly ropey and the mortgage three months in arrears – enough for the lender to commence legal proceedings if they chose to. Thankfully they didn't, but the prospect of losing the roof over our heads lived with us day and night. The bank returned my cheques and would not honour direct debits: health and car insurance and the tax inspector were among the casualties. Fortunately I knew a decent broker who floated me for three months until I could scrape together funds to repay him, and in the meantime I took on night jobs at dance halls to make extra money.

My health started to decline, and the depression was by now well pronounced (though I didn't know so – if only I had taken the time to check my condition with a doctor).

Depression and alcohol fuel each other. It's as if they enjoy a secret pact: one entertains the other, but with a delayed reaction. Alcohol is a depressant, I discovered later, because it suppresses certain chemicals in the brain that raise our moods. Too much alcohol destroys the finely balanced metabolism of the mind–body connections, resulting in anxiety and confusion, anger and sadness, mental and physical disease. Continual alcohol abuse over months and years causes this damage to become both dangerous and irreparable. Paradoxically, depression doesn't feel so bad when you've had a few drinks; but this relief is short-lived. Usually alcohol blurs the mind of a depressed person so much that he or she becomes incapable of logical judgement.

I drank to forget; and the faster I drank, the sooner I achieved the prize. Relief from the pain in my mind and heart was like an anaesthetic blotting out the physical pain of severe toothache. Whenever I drank I could reach a point that seemed to be the perfect balance – but its duration was, of course, short and unsustainable. After a few more drinks I became overwhelmed with sadness and hopelessness.

This might not happen until the following morning, but after a while it started to happen increasingly quickly. Sometimes it would be after I had finished my last drink of the day, or even before I had finished it, and often before I had managed to get myself back home. I would sit in an armchair or lie on the bed – crying, staring at the ceiling or muttering to myself. This was the downside of being able to detach myself from the strings of depression in the pub for a couple of hours.

For a long time I believed that the unbearable sense of worthlessness and utter absence of hope with which I woke up the following morning was merely a bad hangover. I had never had a huge tolerance of alcohol, so I reckoned that I just couldn't get away with drinking as much as some people. Hangovers were very subjective states of mind, I kept telling myself. Everybody's hangover was different.

What I hadn't told myself was that my depression was turning the hangover into a living hell. The more I drank, the more depressed and oppressed I became. I was doing this to myself. The brief respites I had been enjoying from my short visits to the pub stopped and now the depression was there all the time. I felt as though I was riding a bicycle with two flat tyres.

Night-time represented a new terror for me now: sleepless and alone with my thoughts, I couldn't escape the horrors of depression, the terrible boiling anger I felt inside, and the morbid images that flooded my mind. I was terrified for my children, imagining all sorts of terrible catastrophes happening to them. I spent hours thinking about my own funeral, and who might come and what they might say about me as they knelt there paying their final respects. At times it was a comfortable, almost invigorating feeling to know that people would probably be saying nice things about me, as they always do at funerals, whether they meant what they said or not. Whenever I entertained these weird thoughts I felt beyond pain, but eventually I would feel disgusted at the way I had been thinking.

Death seemed to play a role in everything now –

whatever I did had some sort of connection with it. Even music had lost some of its positive power: hearing slow music made me dwell on different aspects of death. And yet, despite its morbidity, it gave me a detached form of comfort, which in turn released me until I found the strength to snap out of this frame of mind that in retrospect never ceased to amaze or frighten me.

During that devastating period of my life I took the decision that somehow I would have to make myself quit drinking. I did so based on my belief that my depression would not lift permanently unless I gave myself enough room to examine clearly what was causing it and to find a way to get it out of my life for good and stop it from ever returning. This may sound like a very tall and perhaps unrealistic order. After all, most medical professionals don't understand depression, despite what they may say to the contrary. If depression research could be compared to Christopher Columbus's voyage to discover America, then I'm afraid he's only just off the west coast of Ireland.

I believe depression is related to moods and emotions. Science might claim that chemical imbalances in the brain are the root of different emotions and moods, and that chemical imbalances cause depressed behaviour. I would turn this back to front. My own experience makes me believe that tangled emotions and low moods, over a prolonged period of time, actually cause those chemical imbalances. Trying to correct a chemical imbalance with a drug is really only removing the symptoms of depression, not its cause. I agree that doctors can change a person's emotional expression by prescribing certain mood-altering drugs, but they will never change the person. You can induce a form of chemical euphoria and well-being by prescribing drugs, but it isn't a natural euphoria.

I can see now that over the years I had been doing something similar with alcohol. I had been inducing a sense of contentment and euphoria, fooling myself into thinking that a few drinks could make me happier and take all my problems away. Instead they simply suppressed the real problems that would need to be dealt with if I was ever going to get beyond this condition that seemed to be getting worse each time it temporarily got a little better.

8

MY BLACKEST NIGHTS

The effects of the alcohol at this time became like a seesaw in my mind. I could never predict how unevenly the seesaw would swing between a comfortable, balanced feeling and one of sheer, hopeless desperation. I could be in the company of friends and suddenly feel the blood drain from my head and body, leaving me gasping for air, sweating and shaking.

On the night when I had my worst experience of this kind, I almost got run over. I arrived in the pub shortly after eight, straight from a long day during which I had had a heated row with a workmate that had left me rankled. I needed to get even – and tomorrow, I decided, I would.

An old friend, an enthusiastic music agent, had called me earlier in the day and asked me to come and listen to his latest band of protégés, destined, he hoped, for fame and the big-time. A couple of small-time promoters and venue owners had also dropped in. The place was packed, the music loud. Usually this was an environment I loved and thrived in – noisy, buzzing, atmospheric, the roof lifting with a couple of hundred watts of raw, jangling rock 'n' roll. Yet from the moment I arrived I knew I didn't want to be there. What I couldn't fathom was *why* I didn't want to be there.

The first drink of the night was always the best,

packing a punch that activated every taste bud and muscle from my front teeth to the back of my throat. But not that night. After one mouthful I put my glass back on the bar and my hand up to my lips. I felt sick. No one seemed to notice.

Soon two old friends whom I hadn't seen for some months joined us. It should have had all the makings of a great night. But, for want of another word that might more aptly describe my uneasiness, I was unwell. I felt more than just tired: I felt wasted. One of our group commented on how heavily I was perspiring. My mouth felt dry, despite the beer. My legs ached. Conversation seemed muffled and distant, with words and questions floating somewhere between my eyes and the faces of my friends. I seemed to be a few seconds behind the discussion, hard pushed to catch the gist of it because of (as I thought) the din from the band belting out familiar numbers at the other end of the room.

The beer flowed all around me. My agent friend was intent on impressing the venue promoters. Talk, as far as I could tell, was about big plans and large venues, seating and ticket prices, commissions and discounts. My own beer still tasted rotten. I watched mouths moving fast, shouting and laughing.

One of our number leaned across and said something to me which he obviously didn't want the rest of the party to hear. I didn't hear it either. I stepped off my bar stool for fear that I would pass out. *This isn't you*, I kept telling myself. I was sick, I was sure of that. I had aches and pains, nausea, a swimming head. Was it flu? A stomach virus? A heart attack? It even occurred to me that perhaps someone had spiked my drink. I had to get out, I decided. Fresh air was what I needed. I grabbed my coat. To this day I cannot remember if I said goodbye to anyone.

As I sat on a bench in the rain outside, someone passing asked if I was OK. I muttered and nodded, stood up and started to move slowly off in the direction of home. I had drunk very little that night, yet I was unable to walk straight. By the time I was halfway home nothing was making much sense. I had a tangy, metallic taste in my mouth. I was shivering, yet at the same time sweating. Stranger still was the sensation in my head. My mind seemed to have shut down, refusing to coordinate my movements. Curiously, I felt an urge to step out in front of the approaching traffic – what would the impact feel like head-on?

By now my coordination and my sense of direction and balance were shattered, my head spinning. Each step was a gargantuan task. If my foot stayed off the ground for a second longer than was absolutely necessary I was convinced I would collapse. The sensations in my head made me think I was suffering from some sort of brainstorm. My clothes were wet through – not from the rain but from my own perspiration. My wrists and ribs and neck ached. My feet felt as though someone had buried them in blocks of concrete. I tried to imagine what I must have looked like as I struggled, with every ounce of strength left in me and every sinew and muscle I could call on, to keep moving forward.

I tried hard to concentrate on one thing – the only thing that mattered at this point: to get home in one piece. Feeling as though I was going to die I started to cry, but no tears were forthcoming. I stumbled along, hands in my pockets, trying to stifle the urge to scream out loud for help. 'Home!' I kept mouthing. 'Home! Home! Home!' With each word I forced myself to take another step. Then I realized I was on the grass verge beside the main road close to my house. I could hear car horns but they seemed to be at a distance. Headlights blinded me. I followed the white line, trying to keep my balance. And then I tripped.

I hit the road so hard that a strange booming bang echoed around my head, and then I could feel the after-shock, like smaller, painful tremors ricocheting around inside my neck and body. I lay there in silence in the darkness, my vision blurred and my face feeling like it had been skinned with a hunting knife. Suddenly the physical pain became unbearable, blotting out all sound and vision – so much so that I never saw the truck.

I recall trying to raise my head to look up, while struggling to free my hands from under my body. The lights felt like floodlights. The truck seemed to be sounding its horn for ever, its huge shape bearing down on me at lightning speed. The screeching of the brakes against the sloshing sounds of the wet road surface grated on my pain and made it ten times worse. Then there was silence, apart from the soft rain falling on my head and stinging the bloody wounds on my face. I heard a door opening and closing, and footsteps, and hard, fast, heavy breathing.

'Can you hear me?' a man asked. 'Don't move. I'll call an ambulance.'

'Don't!' I said. I started to move and he helped me to stand. I mumbled a half-baked apology for scaring him to death, found my bearings and shuffled off home.

Jacqui was so upset she couldn't bear to look at me, so my sister, who lived nearby, came and cleaned me up. Next morning I went down to A & E at the local hospital. Four days later Kerri celebrated her first communion. Needless to say, in the photographs I am the one in the dark glasses. I still wonder what really happened to me that night.

Towards the end of my drinking my mood swings became severe and I was no longer welcome around the house. Bad-humoured and irascible, I was ready to pick silly arguments at any moment of the day or night. I had developed an explosive temper, both frightening and ferocious. At different times I smashed the glass hob of our electric cooker, put my foot through the landing wall and terrified little Kerri who witnessed much of our arguing.

Jacqui, who hated seeing me turn into this monster, had suggested on a number of occasions that I needed to stop, but I just didn't listen to her. She enjoyed a few drinks herself, and I used to think she was a hypocrite for making such a shallow suggestion. We never went anywhere together unless I could get a drink, and then we usually ended up arguing again. In the end it all became too much for our relationship and we couldn't stand being in the same room.

Late one Friday afternoon I left home with a couple of holdalls and moved into a friend's apartment, not wishing to make my wife's life any more miserable than it had already become and anxious to spare my daughters the scars that my current behaviour was likely to leave them with if they witnessed any more of this dreadful physical and mental disintegration. I was away for six weeks. During that time I thought seriously about quitting alcohol and became determined to start a new life for myself. I wasn't sure if my marriage was still intact: Jacqui told me she needed space and time. She also told me she felt it was better if I wasn't in touch with the girls on a daily basis. We had tried to keep our problems within our own four walls, but close friends had been noticing the strain for a long time. It was difficult to see how we were ever going to be able to rebuild our relationship after all we had been through.

My friend's apartment was comfortable but quiet – too quiet. He himself was away, and in this faceless block of flats people didn't mix. I had too much time to myself, and it was a recipe for disaster. Before moving in I had been adamant I was going to stay off the drink, but every evening when darkness began to fall the loneliness drove me to the small, quaint pub across the road. I drank and drank and drank. Most nights I went to bed semi-comatose, often crawling under the duvet fully dressed. I slept until three or four in the morning and would then wake shivering in a cold sweat, shaking from the effects of dehydration and wishing that God would take me at that moment.

I met my wife on a number of prearranged occasions, in places far away from where we might be recognized, and slowly we made plans for me to come back home. We both missed each other and felt, despite the terrible ordeal of the past couple of years, that we really wanted to give it another try.

9

Shortly after my return home a close friend recommended that I should join Alcoholics Anonymous, which had done wonders for him. He had been attending AA for some time, and I noticed how well he looked after only a short time alcohol-free. I remember thinking that I wanted to look as well as he looked, to feel as well as he was telling me he felt. What I saw was a fresh, well-groomed man who seemed totally positive and in control and pointing himself the right way in life. This was everything I wanted for myself.

I had already attempted on a number of occasions to stop drinking, believing I could do so without outside help, but so far it had never worked. I might go for three or four days at a time, a week even, but each time the depression seemed to rise up again and double its strength. I had managed to cut down, but within weeks I found my intake increasing once more. Even so, I knew AA wasn't right for me. Yet I owed it to myself, to Jacqui and the girls to give it a try.

The reason I was unwilling to join AA was that I didn't believe then, and still don't now, that I was an alcoholic. I knew I had become too dependent on the effects of alcohol, but there was no way that my life became unmanageable when I took a few drinks. Many professionals talk in terms of chickens and eggs in this context: some say alcoholism causes depression, while others claim that depression leads to alcoholism. I believe that my depression had been part of my make-up for most of my life, fuelling my low self-esteem and lack of confidence, slowly wearing me down to a level where I found it difficult to convince myself of anything. Alcohol lifted the fog temporarily, and I used it as a crutch when in fact I needed something far more therapeutic and benevolent.

My friend explained to me that right now it was crucial for me to be surrounded by people who did *not* drink – like-minded individuals who, for whatever reason, preferred to abstain from alcohol. The only requirement needed to join AA is the desire to stop drinking. But I had been drawn to alcohol in the way I had because it caused that temporary alleviation of my depression. If I could get beyond depression to a point where it no longer affected my life, I reasoned, then I could also get beyond my habit of drinking to lift it. If my depression lifted permanently, it made perfect sense to me that I would not need to drink in the way that I had been doing. The reason I gave up drinking in the end was not because I had a drink problem, but because I wanted to stop the depression that was slowly stagnating my life, slowly killing me.

I met many wonderful people during my two years attending AA meetings – individuals who had suffered their own nightmares and had come out the other side strong, renewed and full of resolution. Others harboured grudges, never had a good word to say about anyone, nursed bitter memories of the people who had hurt them and shut them out, blamed the world for their problems and spent most of their sobriety talking about their next drink. There were also some who on a number of occasions almost managed to convince me that I was an alcoholic. But the answers I was looking for were not to be found in those rooms. When you walk the walk and talk the talk of AA, it becomes your whole life, and this life exists within a pattern of meetings and a close circle of fellow-AA members who keep you bolstered by always talking the language of the Twelve Step programme. Eventually I left because for me these people were too dogmatic and single-track, unable to accept that not everyone who has a problem with alcohol is an alcoholic. As far as many of these people were concerned, my depression was never regarded as being an adequate excuse to have a few drinks. 'You became depressed because you were alcoholic!' one woman bellowed at me. She was wrong and I knew it.

I stopped drinking for two years, although it had never been my intention to stay off it for a specific length of time – that was just how it shaped out. After a couple of months, it became easier to accept that life could go on without a beer, that my life could be more fruitful and more dynamic if I didn't always dampen my outlook and my creativity with a recipe for deeper depression. It helped me become more coherent and slightly mellower company to be with. I wasn't as antagonistic as before, and tended to listen and chat rather than shout and criticize.

I came to realize that alcohol had only served to compound my already brittle situation. It was fuelling my suffering, thwarting my mind and frustrating the mechanics of my body, which was trying, in its own natural-healing way, to make sense of this senseless condition. I needed help, not alcohol. I needed a programme of recovery and reinvention, not an excuse to prolong the old ways and habits.

It was only after I had quit drinking that I realized how much I had come to depend on its persuasive powers. I was not alcoholic, but I had made an unconscious pact with drink because it raised me above a level where nothing in life made sense. My friends encouraged me to have a drink because it meant they could spend time with me, talking to me, reasoning with me and caring for me; it never worked. I always preferred a couple of quiet drinks on my own, often as soon as I had finished presenting the breakfast show. Even so, the lift I got was so short-lived that I knew long-term I was going to need something far more reliable and durable than a few pints of beer or a bottle of wine to sustain me. Alcohol might see me through a miserable, unending afternoon, helping me eventually to sleep for a couple of hours, but it was not going to help me heal whatever it was inside that was causing me to suffer so.

During my drinking period panic attacks had been regular. My throat would tighten and I would feel an uncontrollable pounding in my chest as if my heart was about to explode. The veins on my neck and arms and on the backs of my hands would stand out starkly, and I would be drenched in sweat as if I had just run a marathon.

I had hoped to say goodbye to these traumatic episodes, but in the weeks immediately after I stopped drinking the panic attacks became very severe. One Saturday morning I was out in a shopping mall with my family and some friends of my daughters when I suddenly became a quivering, shivering wreck. I snapped at the girls because I felt they were walking either too fast or too slowly, or getting in the way of other people, or chatting among themselves and not listening to what I was saying. I treated them as if they were out of control, when in fact it was clearly myself who was out of control. Instead of visiting McDonald's as a treat, which had been our intention, we had to rush back to the car. Scared, I drove home as quickly as I could before my mind cracked with the strain of this paranoia.

But eventually, as with the drinking itself, I learned first to manage and then to overcome these attacks. And once I was post-alcohol a sense of greater acuity and stark awareness entered my life. I felt physically stronger, my appetite increased and I actually looked forward to mealtimes. However, my weight, which had been falling over the past couple of years, continued to drop drastically and rapidly, and it worried me. Was something more sinister at work here?

I joined a gym – not least to fill the empty spaces in the day which previously had been spent in the pub. I lifted weights, walked the treadmill and rode a stationary bike, hoping that this gruelling, boring exercise would increase my appetite still further and help me sleep. I also adopted a high-protein diet, believing that if I could put on muscle I might stop losing weight. But instead of enjoying the sleep of kings, with good skin and a neat physique, I lost four stone in three months, looked wretchedly ill and was deteriorating physically at an alarming rate.

My clothes no longer fitted – even the sleeves of casual sweatshirts and T-shirts hung loosely from my shoulders and dropped down around my elbows, while I had to keep pulling up my trousers to stop them trailing on the ground behind my shoes. My hair was receding at an alarming rate. One morning I went to the barber and asked for the closest haircut he could give me. It made me feel a little better until I looked in the mirror, when I genuinely thought I was dying.

One doctor whom I consulted put it all down to having to get up at four in the morning to present my breakfast show. I knew instinctively he was wrong. I feared that if things continued like this I might have to spend time in hospital. And what if, once I was there, they discovered something serious, like leukaemia or some sort of degenerative muscular disease, that I would be told was terminal? I pushed the idea out of my mind, deciding that, whatever it was, I didn't want a diagnosis. A voice in my head told me that getting a diagnosis would be asking for trouble.

Fortunately, the radio show involved very little preparation. This appealed to me, since I was now barely able to tie my shoelaces. So how did I manage to get through this Jekyll-and-Hyde performance, lurching from total exhaustion to buzzing energy, every day? For one thing, I loved the people I worked with, who helped me to carry the load and made me laugh for that brief part of the day. Secondly, I had a family, and if I failed to entertain what was regarded as the most important audience of the day I would be out of work. I had no choice but to go on microphone and be who my bosses perceived me to be. I owed it to them; they paid me well. Without that salary my family would be homeless, and that notion just didn't bear thinking about.

Jacqui, though pleased to have me back home again and in my new, mellower, post-alcohol state, realized that it could not have been the drink alone that had turned me into a strange, distant alien – that there was something far more deeply rooted affecting my mind and body than a straightforward problem with the bottle. She could no longer bear to hug me because (she told me later) she could feel every rib in my chest and every sharp protruding bone around my waist and hips. If she did throw her arms around me she was terrified my bones might snap.

One Saturday night I went out with friends for a drink – a soft drink – at an old local which I hadn't visited for almost six months. The mere fact that I no longer drank beer made me feel like an outcast. It was clear to me that some of the regulars were visibly uncomfortable chatting at a table with someone holding a glass of bubbly water – someone who only months before would have sat on a bar stool nursing a pint. A woman I hadn't seen for almost two years stopped in her tracks when she saw me sitting there. She sat down opposite me, placed her hand on mine sympathetically and said, 'Jesus Christ, you look as if you've got AIDS!'

Her comment gutted me: I was already raw and she had just poured salt into the wounds. Another evening an acquaintance asked me confidentially if a specialist had checked me out.

'For what?' I asked.

'Cancer,' he replied.

I assured him I didn't have cancer, while deep down a voice was convincing me he might be right.

10

A QUEST FOR ANSWERS

Almost a year before my depression was properly diagnosed I went to a doctor for help because, despite the absence of alcohol now, there was still this terrible difference between the way I was experiencing my life and the way people around me were experiencing theirs. I had cut off the source of what I believed had caused me to feel so miserable, so why was I feeling ten times worse and looking so deathly? Why, if the root cause of my hopelessness had been removed, was I not feeling wonderful and hopeful and optimistic?

The doctor – a new one, not the one I had previously consulted – told me that over the years I had become too reliant on alcohol and, despite giving up, the effects were still with me. He never mentioned depression, but suggested a course of Prozac 'to see what happens'. I told him I didn't want Prozac. He asked if I would like to talk to a psychiatrist. He was 'well connected' and knew a couple of good ones. I still wasn't sure why I should want to talk to a psychiatrist. I just wanted energy, I told him.

I found it odd that he had never heard of the popular herbal antidepressant St John's Wort. Having read about it, I had been taking it to treat the way I was feeling. But it was no longer available over the counter in health food stores, and could now only be obtained on prescription from a pharmacy. 'Spell it for me,' he said, as he wrote out a new prescription.

It still strikes me as strange that I could take something that was clearly labelled as a remedy for depression and yet not admit to myself that what I was suffering from was indeed very likely to be depression. I told myself I felt down, very down – I was depressed, yes; but I never articulated that word 'depression'. I wanted something light and easy that I could fool myself into thinking was giving me partial relief from the way I felt. If I kept taking something for it there was bound to be some relief at some stage, I told myself. I just had to be patient.

Perhaps this persistent denial might explain why so many sufferers remain on prescribed medication for years rather than trying to tackle the underlying causes. Antidepressants work in much the same way, broadly speaking, as painkillers – they remove the symptoms, not the cause of the problem. And when a ship sinks, survivors will cling to anything that keeps them afloat and alive. The doctor prescribed Xanax to help me relax and asked me again if I wanted Prozac. I still said no to Prozac but took the Xanax, a powerful sedative with strong tranquillizing effects that arrived in my life like manna from heaven. It helped me sleep, relax and breeze through the day without a care in the world, as if I was permanently wrapped in warm cotton wool. Yet some- where deep down inside I knew it was also wrong. After three weeks I made a difficult decision and weaned myself off the Xanax, because I knew what would happen if I didn't. I couldn't remember a time before that when I had even taken paracetamol for a headache, so I was damned if I was going to risk getting hooked on tranquillizers.

The first few days were horrible, cold and stark as the cushioning effect was replaced by the all too familiar confusion and the morose, morbid thinking returned with a vengeance. Everything was back to being hellish and upsetting and anger-inducing. I wondered if I should look for yet another doctor. There had to be someone out there who could help me make better sense of this nightmare.

Despite Jacqui's pleas, I never went outside the front door if I didn't have to. Apart from presenting my daily radio show, I remained housebound in order to muster up the necessary strength for each two-hour early morning stint. Restaurants, bars, clubs and weekends away were for other people. Family and friends were locked out. I didn't want to see them because I felt I had nothing to say to them any more, nothing in common with any of them, nothing they could possibly understand.

There was, however, one thing I could turn to at those moments when I could summon up the mental energy. Back in 1995 I had returned to an early love from my childhood, the English language, and started to write fiction, using the PC that was sitting idly in the corner of the dining room, a redundant relic of our abortive business venture with the children's books. Two years later my first novel, *Dare to Die*, had been published and reached number two in the *Irish Times* bestseller list. When I wrote I didn't have to abide by the rules that governed everyday life: I was in charge. My fiction had become my means of expression, an outlet for the pain and confusion in my life. Not surprisingly, once again I now buried myself in inventing characters and concocting storylines. But mostly, it has to be said, I slept.

Many people who have suffered from depression refer to 'the demons', the tormenting, crushing thoughts and demands that persecute them for no apparent reason. My own demons slowly started to take me apart, to dismantle me covertly like skin flaking away in the days and weeks following a good suntan.

At this time my depression followed a peculiar pattern. As I described earlier, the demons usually reached their peak in the early to mid-afternoon. Between midday and four my life dissolved into anarchy, a meaningless mesh of muddled thinking, frightening mind flashes and a sense of hopelessness that's difficult to describe accurately because it etched away at my focus and acuity. In short, I cannot remember much about these bleak afternoons that, over a three-year period, often almost scared me to death. Perhaps that was the main reason why, when I was still drinking, I chose to do so at lunchtime, to counter the onslaught of the physical misery with some kind of anaesthetic effect.

Despite the afternoons of pure hell, for some inexplicable reason the gruesome pain lifted somewhat at twilight, and from about six until whatever time I chose to go to bed I would feel reasonably well again. I use the word 'reasonably' because it never fully went away during those three years.

By seven each evening I felt relaxed and safe again, as though I'd scaled the north face of the Eiger. On particularly bad afternoons the evening would feel like a place beyond the horizon – out of sight and out of reach. On good evenings, as I sat and escaped into my music, I often silently congratulated myself for once again beating the demons, for bravely clinging to life and in doing so giving myself just a little chink of hope. The evenings when I felt hope were the evenings when I was glad to be still alive.

Night-time, however, brought nightmares. I never slept for longer than half an hour at a time, concocting vicious dreams that ate into the important sleep rhythm. I know now that depression is associated with excessive amounts of what is called REM (rapid eye movement) sleep, which usually occurs just after falling asleep and again just before waking. REM activity is an indication that dreaming is taking place, and a certain amount is perfectly normal. However, too much dreaming prevents us attaining the deeper sleep we all require to allow the body and mind to recharge themselves. I used to wake each morning feeling drained and exhausted. Sleep became my enemy.

People often ask me if Jacqui was supportive during those awful days. I have no doubt she was, but the truth is that I don't remember much about that time. It's as if part of my mind kept me at a distance in order to protect me. The demons can reach such unfathomable depths and cause such excruciating pain that words cannot describe the misery. The good news is that such heart-breaking, life-destroying pain *does* go away completely, *does* become part of the past and remain so, once recovery starts to take hold of your life. But for me, this still lay in the future.

Now that I no longer drank, and had stopped taking

tranquillizers, my mind was painfully clear and sharp all the time. I tried to burn off that stark clarity by reading. I had bought a book by Frieda Fordham called *An Introduction to Jung's Psychology*, about the great Swiss psychiatrist Carl Gustav Jung. Jung had endured severe depression and anxiety and had spent time in hospital. However, he recovered quite rapidly and seemed to develop an uncanny insight into the psychology of the spiritual mind as distinct from the chemical workings of the brain. I reckoned that if he had studied the mind so intensely following his 'aberration' perhaps he had also found a way of healing his depression.

Jung spoke about the power of the unconscious mind and how it governed the whole body–mind system, and in particular about what he called the collective unconscious. What he meant is that every person's mind is connected to a great stream of collective thought that spans centuries of time, and that each of us is influenced and shaped by every thought that has ever been created by every mind that has ever existed. At first I found this notion absurd, but I persisted and read more and started to search for that elusive meaning. Maybe Jung's ideas would help to explain something about my own condition.

Around this time, being alone so much, I had also started to pray a little. I prayed to a power which I believed existed both within me and outside of me. Little else existed now; little made sense. I knew that if I refused to believe in something much greater than me, life would no longer be worth living. However, if there was something both out there *and* inside me, something that could transcend this unbearable state of being, something that could at the end of the day make me see that there was sense, that there was a specific reason for my suffering and enduring this pain, then maybe I could get beyond it once I had learned what it had been trying to teach me. I desperately wanted to believe that whatever was going on within me had a purpose: perhaps huge changes were required in my life and in the way I had been living. Did this sense of loss represent an old life dying, and was I standing somewhere in the middle waiting for the new life to be born? Some days this idea made perfect sense; on others it was pure nonsense. However, on the days it made sense I always felt a hugely comforting strength that offered me a lifeline of hope and encouraged me to hang on and listen to what these thoughts and feelings were saying to me.

I knew I needed a complete change of direction, but how was I going to do that? Was it even possible now, in my late thirties? Anything was possible, I always used to remind myself. It was easy to say when everything was going swimmingly, of course, but another matter altogether when the storm clouds had gathered and the circumstances were difficult. I was married, with three young daughters and a large mortgage. I couldn't just leave my job and go and live with nature in the Amazon rainforest for six months in order to learn more about myself. Each time I applied my mind to the subject of change I rapidly became exhausted. How could I change without changing? This was the six million dollar question I kept putting to myself. I was waiting for answers, but how could I be sure that the messages of hope I occasionally glimpsed were not just the effect of my weak, wrecked and confused head playing mind games with me? The challenge seemed, for the present, insurmountable.

11

BREAKING THE TABOO

On a beautiful, warm, sunny morning I was busy writing a chapter of my novel *The Limbo Vigil*, when the telephone rang. It was not good news. Derek, a close friend, had killed himself. He had been diagnosed as suffering from clinical depression, had spent two periods in a psychiatric hospital and had just been asked to consider another spell there. He and I had known for some time that we both had problems. Some weeks earlier I had come across him in a shop and tried to talk to him in an effort to forge a bond to fight this together, to lean on each other, to compare notes on what might work and what might not. But he chose not to respond that day, and I chose to respect his privacy. Perhaps I shouldn't have. All I wanted to say was that I understood, that I too was feeling much the same. It might have helped. It might not. I shall never know.

While preparing this book I spent a long time considering whether or not to write at some length about suicide. As I explained in the Introduction, suicidal feelings and attempted suicide frequently accompany depression, and the numbers of people who actually do commit suicide are rising. So in the end I decided this important subject merited a chapter on its own. Until I went researching, I had never realized quite so many books had been written on suicide. I tracked down a number of them for the purpose of educating my own perspective on just what it might be that finally pushes someone over the edge – feelings that I entertained, on and off, throughout my years of depression. Nearly all these accounts make for grim, upsetting reading; one of them left me feeling devastated for days after finishing it.

Part of me feels there is only so much that can be written about suicide, while another part of me feels there needs to be more – more research, more understanding. It's one of the great paradoxes of suicide that, while few people can bear to talk about it, those who write about it don't seem too sure about who they should be addressing their work and research to. The problem is that for those who contemplate suicide it remains a closely guarded secret, while for those left behind it becomes impossible to accept. No one knows until it's too late. Of course, not all depressed people become suicidal, nor are all the people who commit suicide depressed – another of the great contradictions of this disorder.

So what are the merits of discussing a subject that remains improper and dirty and frowned upon in our society? To rid it of its label of indecency and to raise it above the level of vulgar whispering and out into the open would be a good start. To discuss depression without referring to suicide is a bit like thunder without lightning; and if thunder can be likened to a distant sign of approaching depression, then the lightning often catches us unaware when it does strike – not unlike suicide. On the other hand, it is often too painful and sensitive a subject, especially for partners and families who have lost loved ones.

I believe the reason that suicide is so difficult to talk about is that we know so little about it and, if we are involved in whatever capacity, end up feeling helpless and guilty. Most people who have lost friends or family members in this way feel the blame rests partly on themselves for not having paid attention to whatever signs they might have spotted if only they had been more vigilant. *If only we could have got him to talk more . . . If only we had been more gentle and patient . . . If only we had been less selfish with our time . . . If only we had listened . . . If only, if only, if only . . .*

Suicide has to be talked about, if only to shine some light on why it continues to claims its victims like Derek and to pinpoint why those closest to the victim should not blame themselves for something for which, in the end, no one can be held responsible. Having said that, as one who has been to the edge but stopped short of jumping I must add that I do not condone suicide. It is pointless and irrational, an act of despair and not an act of courage. Nor is it a dignified act. Someone who takes their own life wants not to die so much as to stop the pain they are enduring alone. They know no other way, but this way is too final. In killing themselves they are relinquishing what few vestiges of control still remain to them, glimmers of hope that, unknown to their weary minds, might have been softly pleading for just one more try. Suicide is a permanent solution to a temporary problem.

'Metastasis' is a word which many cancer sufferers will

be familiar with – a word that strikes fear into the minds of patients and their families. When a cancer metastasizes it spreads at lightning speed, usually with devastating effect, unless it can be stopped rapidly. Depression in its severest form is like cancer. Suicide is often the result of the depression metastasizing throughout the entire system, body and mind, to the point where the desire to put an end to this invisible, crippling pain outweighs everything else. The will to live is too agonizing to contemplate.

At this point the mind sends out a message to the limbic system – the mechanism in the body which deals with emotional control but which is now, as a result of the depression, overwhelmingly distorted – that this terrible pain must be stopped. That message goes out to millions of cells. They comply. Before the act of suicide is ever perpetrated, the body has already started a process known by pathologists as 'surcease'. What it means is total shutdown. And this, I believe, succinctly describes the immediate catalyst that drives people to suicide.

The lure of suicide is like the mirage of an oasis to a man who is lost in the desert, having gone without water for days. In his mind it is real, offering him a picture of what he wants to see. The problem is that it is a horrible distortion – one he fails to see through. He may at first wonder if he is 'seeing things' – but then again, what if he isn't? What if this beautiful, shiny, shimmering vision in the distance *is* real? He feels he would be mad not to investigate it – just to be sure in his own mind that he isn't hallucinating. And what if he *is* mad? Who cares? Isn't it better to have something to look forward to, even if it does turn out to be an illusion? The illusion will take his mind off his unbearable thirst – or, in the case of someone with depression, off his pain, anguish, confusion, desperation, loneliness and sheer exhaustion. This holographic image, by which the sun plays tricks on the unconscious mind's inability to perceptualize, can include friends and family, boss and workmates – even public and historical figures can make a guest appearance. The mind is both a miracle and a menace.

Maybe the oasis isn't real, but what if it is a reflection of 'better things' beyond the next sand dunes? If he doesn't satisfy his curiosity, he reasons, he will never know. Given his overwhelming desire for relief from the burning sun in the cool shade of the palm trees, and for the taste of ice-cold water from a deep desert well, it makes perfect sense to head in that direction right now.

But what if the oasis lies the other way? Just one more sand dune and then he'll know for sure. At this point he looks back to satisfy his curiosity: all he can see is sand and more sand. He can't even rationalize the notion that he may just be heading deeper into the desert, which is usually the case with a mirage.

Seeing birds flying in the direction he has just come from should have made him turn round and go back, but no – the mirage is now reality. He doesn't care about anything any more, only the relief that cool water and shade will bring him. His eyes and brain collude to convert the loose distant image into a tangible object of desire, growing clearer by the minute. He has reached the point of no return, and no one and nothing can stop him.

Suicide is the ultimate act of will in a faulty and warped process of self-vindication. *No one can accuse me of any wrongdoing to anyone else*, runs the argument in the intending suicide's mind, *because I have decided to do it all by myself. I have only myself to blame. It is my own free will that has decided on this course of action*. It represents freedom from a dark, windowless cell of sadness, anger, self-loathing and the sense of worthlessness. Suicide sprouts wings when nothing else – absolutely nothing that ever held importance and had a sense of hopeful structure – makes any sense. At that terrible moment suicide seems to have more going for it, in the eyes of its victims, than the nothingness of hopelessness and the prospect of an eternity of invisible pain and suffering.

Why does someone who commits suicide hate himself so much? A woman put this question to me some weeks after her husband had killed himself. 'I loved him with everything I had, everything I was. I gave him as much as I could and more. Why was he so selfish that he could hate himself so much? Why couldn't he have tried to love me and the kids more, like we loved him? Why has he left me to carry all the pain now?'

I believe that someone on the brink of the abyss has forsaken everything. He has no self-respect, for he no longer understands what self-respect is. He has abandoned awareness in all its guises. And he has relinquished the very essence of what it means to be loved, the selfless will to love back, and the wholesomeness of the dignity and esteem he once cherished. In many ways, death has already occurred long before the sufferer commits the final act.

Some of the great psychiatrists of our time, such as Aaron Beck, Kay Redfield Jamison and Harvey Resnik, have spent many years studying the subject of suicide, trying to discover why people take their own lives, attempting to identify signs and symptoms in the preceding days and weeks in the hope that the rest of us can become more watchful and offer fresh hope. While I was recovering from my own depression, and since, I read many of their books. They explained a lot about the 'types' of at-risk individuals, based on such things as their family background, relationship difficulties, mental state, occupational leanings and other possible triggers, but nothing in any of these books has satisfied my curiosity as to why these people see the desire to commit suicide through to the bitter end.

Although suicide remains a shocking concept, in recent years the subject has attracted interest from both academics, who are devoting more time and money to research, and from various religious organizations and charities. However, some old myths still need to be blown out of the water.

Myth 1: people who commit suicide go to hell. This is what some people with strong religious convictions believe – but I don't, any more than I believe that pigs can fly. I like to believe that we are watched over by a forgiving, loving God, who understands the delicate nature of human existence. Suicide is not a sin. In order to sin, we have to be thinking logically and deviously. Someone who is on the brink of suicide is neither of these. For me, a priest summed it all up during the sermon he preached at the funeral mass of a friend of mine who had killed himself: 'Michael decided he just wanted to go home,' he said. This, I felt, was a fitting and loving judgement on the end of a life that had been gentle, generous and gifted. I believe that, while God might not have called this man home, he still held out his loving arms to him when he arrived unexpectedly on the doorstep.

Myth 2: most suicides occur during the dark, short days of winter. This belief is probably associated with our primitive fear of darkness and dislike of wet, cold weather. In fact statistics show that, with the exception of Christmas and New Year, a trying time for most people – problem family relationships for some, loneliness for others, financial demands on everyone – most suicides take place in early summer, in May and June. No one knows why. Some experts have suggested it might have something to do with biological changes connected with the rhythm of the seasons. I believe it is because the desire for suicide is more manageable in winter, when nature appears frozen and static, whereas when everything round about is growing and flowering the potential suicide remains frozen out by his deep and relentless desire to die.

Myth 3: you have to be depressed to commit suicide. As I said earlier, no you don't. Suicide is a declaration of emotional bankruptcy. For this situation to arise, you don't have to exhibit the signs and symptoms of depression. Sudden bereavement, losing your job, being declared bankrupt, finding out your partner is sleeping with your best friend, failing important exams, being bullied by your boss or something as simple as having an argument with your lover – all these, and many more scenarios besides, are capable of sending a person over the edge. The reason why people who are not depressed kill themselves is that their familiar worlds have become so radically changed in a very short space of time that they no longer feel included or, more importantly, in control. In his book *The Savage God* the well-known English writer and critic A. Alvarez calls this form of death 'anomic suicide'. It is 'the result of a change in a man's social position so sudden that he is unable to cope with his new situation'.

As long ago as 1955 Peter Sainsbury, in his pioneering study *Suicide in London*, showed that someone who is excluded from their normal social environment and left to contend with pure loneliness is more likely to kill himself or herself than someone who is suffering from what he called 'indigenous poverty'. So – perhaps surprisingly in some people's eyes – the woman who wins a million in the lottery is more likely to commit suicide than her counterpart who is bringing up eight children on her own and has to borrow from loan sharks in order to feed them. Social aggression, keeping up appearances, peer pressure, impossible expectations, suddenly finding ourselves out of the social circle we were accustomed to moving in, lack of structure, loss of principles, a sudden absence of the internal code of ethics by which we have always unconsciously lived our lives – these are all classic states, or mind fields, that lead to despair, hopelessness and a failure to see anything better emerging on the horizon.

Myth 4: people who commit suicide usually have it

planned well in advance. This is not true – or, at least, those who have attempted suicide and survived say it is not. Many people believe that the mood of depressed sufferers often improves two to three weeks before the act of suicide, sometimes to the point of euphoria; this leads friends and family to believe that their loved one is getting better. That, too, is a myth. Most suicides are spur-of-the-moment, with perhaps two or three days contemplating the act itself. Finally, the person in question is supposed to get his affairs in order – paying bills, leaving important addresses and telephone numbers where they can easily be found by others, and so on. Again, not so. People who decide to die are unusually stealth-like in everything they do in the days and hours leading up to their final act, for fear that someone might find out and stop them.

Myth 5: people who kill themselves never consider those whom they leave behind. I believe this could not be further from the truth. Those who kill themselves usually love their family and friends so much they often think that by dying they are doing them a good turn. The need to stop the pain is filled with frustration, exasperation, anger and self-loathing. Mix in profound loneliness and impenetrable hopelessness and you have a lethal concoction.

Suicide is not selfish for the perpetrator. It might appear so to the perpetrator's husband, wife or partner, left behind to pick up the pieces and perhaps bring up traumatized children alone. For the perpetrator, their death was an act of charity, as they understood it: they were doing their wife, let us say, a favour, allowing her to free herself from this dark prison to which he had committed her as a result of his suffering. Someone who is on the brink of suicide has lost the true meaning of what were once their most important values. Love, kind thoughts, generosity and other major emotions still exist, but not as other people know them; now their meaning has become twisted.

Despite exploding these myths and exposing them for the old wives' tales they really are, suicide is still a dirty word to most people. Nothing can ever prepare us for such a cruel ending to a loved life. I don't know many people who are comfortable discussing suicide in general, let alone discussing a particular person who has done so. I can talk about it, but every few minutes I have to stop and breathe deeply and remind myself how good my life is today, and how wonderful the person we are talking about really was. Then I have to remember that person and see in him all the love he gave us and all the things that he stood for to those he left behind.

So how can suicide be prevented? It is not always possible to anticipate the breakdown of a relationship or a business failure, but in the case of suicidally depressed people we can make sure we understand what causes the states of mind that make the pain too great for the sufferer to bear. By understanding depression we can change it into something more productively healing, and in so doing prevent such life-threatening pain from getting an irreversible hold on the lives of people we love.

80

12

THE BEGINNINGS OF HOPE

In the days after the suicide of my kind, gentle friend Derek, a tower of strength and a source of inspiration to everyone who knew him well, my own life finally seemed to crumble. The ability to manage my depression and the understanding of suicide still lay in the future. Without such knowledge and self-confidence I regularly contemplated suicide myself, trying to think of the quickest, most painless ways to put an end to this mess.

Morbid, hellish thoughts filled my mind, striking without warning like small electric shocks. I cried and begged for this misery, this brainwashing, to end. My brain itself seemed to have turned to mush and my creativity and initiative – qualities I had never been short of throughout my life – had gone. For hours at a time the damp, empty attic that was my mind dwelt on where Derek had gone. Was he happy? Had his desperate action been worth it? Yet, despite the devastating confusion, something deep within me was convincing me that it was not worth dying for – that I should not follow in his footsteps and end it all.

I was desperate for tablets that would help me sleep, help me shut out the world and take me somewhere I could be comfortably numb. I started to take Xanax again. It was an easy option, one that I knew was not a good choice – but what the hell.

My wife could no longer cope with what was happening as I slowly disintegrated before her eyes. I felt too isolated now even to appreciate her caring nature; only at a much later date would I be able to look back and do so. And yet it was thanks to Jacqui, though indirectly, that at last I started to get some answers. Bizarrely, my life changed because of an unfortunate back injury she sustained one weekend while gardening.

The following morning she was unable to get out of bed. The more she twisted, the more excruciating the pain in her back and leg became. I rang our family doctor, Michael, whom we had known for years, and asked if he could call. I felt a little uncomfortable talking to him as I had been taking myself off to other doctors in the past few years. But I had since regretted my decision, and now wondered if Michael might consider taking me back.

When he came downstairs again after examining Jacqui I asked him, 'Is she going to be OK?' I shall never forget his reply.

'Oh, she's going to be fine. It's you I'm worried about.' He asked me to sit down and posed a number of questions, to each of which I answered a definitive yes. 'Just as I'd suspected. I think you're suffering from severe depression, and have been for a good while, and it's been gradually getting worse and worse. Jacqui has confirmed my suspicions. You haven't been right for a long time, Gareth.'

I thought about each word he had just spoken, and one

in particular: depression. Perhaps I needed to hear someone with professional credentials say this to me. It might
not have had the same effect if my wife had said it. Or
maybe she had already said it, and I just hadn't heard it.

I often wondered what it might feel like to be told by a
doctor that I was seriously ill. It felt different from what I
had thought it might feel like. But *was* I seriously ill? Was
depression a serious illness? Although it was a huge relief
to hear this final confirmation that I had depression, I
still preferred not to think that I was seriously ill.

'There's no need to be upset by all this,' Michael went
on. 'I think we'll put you on a course of medication and
get you back to your old self again. What do you think?'

I was flabbergasted, shocked, terrified, dismayed and
relieved – all at the same time. Something deep inside had
clicked. It was as if he had found the combination,
cracked the code and unlocked the safe in which my life
had been locked up. I felt energy surge through me like a
breath of cool, fresh air. His suggestion of medication
also came as a relief, unlike the previous doctor's offer of
Prozac. Perhaps first time round I wasn't ready to admit
that I needed heavy-duty help – that, yes, I was badly in
need of supervised assistance. Doctors play a huge role in
determining the outcome of a person's well-being. Almost a year earlier another doctor had suggested a course
of medication for suspected depression, not unlike the
one I was now about to start; yet it took a different man's
perspective to get me to accept that there was something
radically wrong with the way I was living my life.

Those gentle, life-saving, reassuring words that I heard
that Saturday morning made me feel more grateful than

anything anyone had ever said to me before. I sometimes wonder what direction my life might have taken had I not called Michael to look at my wife's injury that morning. As it was, something positive was at last taking place in my life.

Our discussion revealed a glimpse of how things could be, which in time became the basis for the hard work and total commitment I would put into my own recovery. I know now that this foundation does not have to be laid by a doctor, or by any other medical professional for that matter, but can be laid by anyone who is equipped with the right tools. With hindsight, I can distinguish five things that emerged from that morning's conversation which unconsciously changed the way I was feeling. They started to redirect my attitude to this state of mind called depression and, consequently, to my outlook on the life I so desperately wanted to live.

First, Michael approached me as a friend. Many people with depression (myself included, of course) don't talk to a doctor, or indeed anybody, because, as I have explained, they have very little understanding of just what it is that's wrong with them. Facing up to their emotional crisis is a task that overwhelms their already weakened resolve. They feel incapable of performing even the smallest tasks, such as showering and caring for their appearance, so to get a grasp on what's going on within them seems impossible. When Michael approached me that morning it was in a friendly, non-confrontational way, and in so doing he held out a helping hand. When I realized that he was doing this, the sheer release and relief were wonderful.

Secondly, he reassured me. I know now that I badly needed to be told that I was not cracking up, that I was not beyond help, that there was no need to be ashamed or disgusted by the way I was feeling about my life. My distorted, painful thinking was the result of tangled emotions and confused moods caused by this invisible cloud. As he explained each stage of depression, he continued to reassure me with positive talk and suggestions.

Thirdly, there was an unexpected acceptance on his part. I never felt that my behaviour would have been acceptable to anyone. Yet Michael accepted that this was what depression had done to me – he accepted that I should not be blaming myself for the direction my life had taken me in.

Fourthly, I became equipped with the knowledge I needed. People who suffer depression are often afraid to ask questions because we are ashamed of what we are becoming. The voice of low self-esteem tells us that this is the way we deserve to be; that by asking stupid questions we may only worsen an already delicate issue. In the space of half an hour that morning I learned about what was wrong with me. Even if the details made little sense at that point, at least I now knew I could get well.

Fourthly, Michael showed me empathy. Sympathy is affectionate support, or a way of communicating agreement or understanding, whereas empathy is something much greater and more seldom encountered. Empathy is the power and ability to enter into the spirit of someone else's deepest pain but without appearing intrusive. Someone who is empathic really understands what's wrong, as opposed to someone who just mimics the hurt and throws out bargain-bin sympathy.

Empathy is not a natural gift that comes at birth in our gene package. It is not a sixth sense or some arcane power. You don't have to be a former sufferer from depression to be able to show empathy to someone who is lost in a private hell. Empathy can be learned and honed so that you can show it without realizing it. Its four mainstays are to befriend (don't be afraid you might be intruding – reach out and show you care); to accept (don't criticize, don't analyse, just accept); to reassure (listen, gently raise self-esteem and confidence, and don't say, 'I know' if you don't); and finally to be open (if someone who has been depressed for a long time wants to discuss matters that seem shocking or upsetting, remember that this is the depression talking, not the person, and that being open will help to rid the person's mind of these painful feelings).

The power of empathy cannot be underestimated. If I know someone can reach that far into me, I won't be able to resist the hopefulness stirred by that gesture. Empathy is the secret ingredient that underlies hope. With hope comes healing, and once the healing begins life takes on a whole new meaning.

Fifthly, having the right doctor or therapist is vital. Many people go to the same doctor for years simply because it is convenient for them. Or maybe he or she is the only doctor in their local community. In some places it can be difficult to get on to a doctor's list at all, and once on it you don't want to compromise your position by looking elsewhere.

But in the case of depression, or suspected depression, it really is worth the effort of tracking down the right doctor. The approaches they favour vary widely. Some will just prescribe a course of antidepressant medication, which is no good unless the doctor also informs you precisely what to expect in the days, weeks and months ahead, and whether or not you can expect to recover fully. Others will tell you that the depression will lift on its own if you are patient and give it time, which is unlikely. Many will tell you, quite rightly, that there are plenty of quick-fix therapists and inexperienced coun-sellors out there who will be only too happy to part you from your money in return for a 'guaranteed cure'.

I was so lucky to have Michael at hand. If you aren't as happy with your doctor as I was with mine, ask your friends and neighbours for recommendations. Rapport in a patient–doctor relationship is crucial, especially for those with depression. One fellow depression sufferer asked me, 'What's the difference between the Samaritans and my GP?'

'I don't know,' I said. 'Tell me.'

'At least the Samaritans listen to what I have to say,' was his chilling reply. He was obviously one of the unlucky ones.

I believe my doctor is interested not only in my health but in my uncertainties, my welfare and, consequently, my happiness. I can open up to this man, tell him things I perhaps wouldn't feel comfortable telling my best friend because she might feel embarrassed or get upset. For most people the notion of telling their partner they are feeling suicidal is inconceivable, but telling that to your doctor is one of the things he is there for. By sharing with my doctor I have unburdened myself of half the problem; usually the other half can be solved in his replies to my questions. I call him Michael. He calls me Gareth. We don't have meals in each other's houses, nor do we all go away for family weekends together. The point I am making is that I wouldn't feel uncomfortable if we *did* have a meal together. That's what rapport means. Without rapport, there can be no hope. And without hope, there will be no improvement in your situation.

13

EFFECTS AND SIDE-EFFECTS

What Michael prescribed for me was an antidepressant called Cipramil, one of the newer mood-altering wonder drugs in the range of medications called Selective Serotonin Reuptake Inhibitors – more commonly known, understandably, as SSRIs. Serotonin is often known as the 'happy hormone': it is an essential chemical, manufactured in the brain, that creates feelings of well-being, contentment and balance in us. But in some people the process is faulty, and they need SSRIs to prevent the serotonin they produce from being reabsorbed by the brain and causing a serious lack of balance. Michael explained that it would be four to six weeks before the medication really kicked in, although I might see the odd improvement after a fortnight or so.

When I mentioned the herbal antidepressant I had been taking, St John's Wort, his jaw dropped. The doctor I had previously consulted hadn't heard of it, but Michael knew all about it – more than I did, it seemed.

'How long have you been taking that?' he asked.

'Almost a year,' I replied. 'I thought it might help when things began to go from bad to worse, but I think I've just been fooling myself.'

He explained that research had shown it to be beneficial for some people who suffer from mild depression, but that scientists were still at a loss as to why it worked on some people and not on others. He stared down at the prescription he had just written out, and my heart sank as I sensed there was something wrong. Feelings of worthlessness and pessimism started to crowd in.

'Is there a problem, Michael?' I asked.

'In the short term, yes – a big problem. This is a very dangerous mixture to be juggling with. Research is beginning to show that blood pressure and all sorts of troubles, like heart problems for instance, can arise if you mix these different concoctions. And that's the difficulty with herbal medication. It's early days in terms of re-search into these alternative treatments. They're still not sure what these remedies are capable of doing inside your head.' He took back the prescription. 'I'm afraid you won't be able to start the Cipramil for at least another five weeks – not until you give your system a chance to flush out the herbal stuff.'

Five weeks! I felt I wasn't getting a look in here. Was I not meant to recover *ever*? As Michael tore up the prescription he looked as disappointed as I felt.

'Best thing we can do is just keep in touch, and let's hope the five weeks will pass quickly for you.'

Even five hours was too long to contemplate, the way I was feeling. It seemed like an eternity. *Just think*, I kept telling myself, *in five days I'm still going to be feeling the same way*. How was I ever going to manage five weeks? And even then, once I had started on the proper medica-tion it would be another four weeks before anything positive started to show up. Surely I would just collapse under the strain of it all?

As I feared, it was not an easy period of waiting and the days dragged heavily. Needless to say, I stopped taking the St John's Wort straightaway. I was going cold turkey and felt every bit of it, which convinced me that my herbal remedy must have been doing me some good. I definitely experienced a period of detox which I wouldn't recommend to my worst enemy. But I knew it was only a matter of time and I did at least have something to focus on now: the opportunity to feel well again. It raised my mood, if only slightly. I tried to imagine what it might feel like, tried to construct an image of what I was going to be like. But interspersed with these more positive moments were horrific days when everything seemed to slip out of reach again. To this day I don't know for sure what, if any, were the therapeutic effects on me of the herbal remedy I had been taking.

To help me get through this limbo period Michael had prescribed a light sleeping pill called Noctamid, for which I was grateful. I didn't really like the idea of taking them, because I realized they could become addictive and I had already had a difficult fortnight weaning myself off Xanax. But I took these and as a result slept soundly most nights, which gave me more energy the following day.

When I was only about ten days away from the end of the limbo period I had one terrible afternoon when I felt that I was seriously losing my mind. The house was empty. Alone and very frightened, I broke into a sweat. In panic I picked up the phone, intending to plead with Michael to let me have the Cipramil prescription *now*. But it was a Saturday and he had finished for the weekend, so I could only leave a message. Worse, it was a bank holiday weekend so I probably wouldn't hear from him until the following Tuesday – and that, to me, was a lifetime away.

I was lucky – he rang back that evening. Eventually, after I had assured him many times over that I would take full and total responsibility for any consequences to my heart and my health in general, he agreed to let me have my prescription. That evening I ran into the pharmacy waving my precious bit of paper as if it was a winning lottery ticket. I felt like celebrating. I wanted to believe that I had reached the crossroads and was about to turn down the road signposted 'recovery'.

Around this time, too, something else was happening to me that in the long term was far more significant than medication in terms of my journey out of depression. During this strange period of waiting, my firm belief that the start of that journey was only a few weeks away had stirred something inside me: a determination to survive. I told myself repeatedly that all I needed to do was hold on, because now I had something concrete and reliable to focus on. This was what began to give me hope, and hope was the essential ingredient in my recovery.

I also believe that intuition played a big part in getting me to that stage. Who had made the decision that I was going to get better? It wasn't my doctor, although he had been hugely instrumental. It wasn't my family, although they had helped me to hang on for dear life. The decision was mine. I had behaved intuitively – my mind had instinctively chosen the right path to take, without in-dulging in reason or analysis of the alternatives. And my intuition was now rewarding me by very slowly giving me the strength I needed to take back control of my own life. Later, during my convalescence, I realized what a huge role intuition had played in making me well. It is central to the way the body–mind heals any setback that we suffer, and I shall return to it in Chapter 14.

Sadly, after all the hope and optimism and the interminable waiting, it turned out to be too good to be true. After four weeks on Cipramil I had a horrendous reaction. I itched, sweated and shivered violently, became increasingly nervous and paranoid, and at one point my heart was beating so fast and furiously I thought it was going to explode. When I consulted Michael he told me I had Serotonin Syndrome, a reaction caused by too much of the substance circulating in my blood. And the cause of it? In an attempt to put back some of my lost weight, twice a day for a couple of months I had been taking a high-protein drink; unfortunately, one of its ingredients assisted the brain to produce serotonin. In short, I had overdosed.

So it was off the Cipramil and on to another antidepressant, Prothiaden, one of the older, tricyclic types of drug that had been around since the mid-1960s. I could take it straightaway, Michael assured me, without any 'cooling off' period after stopping the Cipramil. Tricyclics are reckoned to have a wonderful 60–70 per cent success rate in alleviating the symptoms of depression, and indeed the Prothiaden worked for me after another four-week delay until it kicked in. But there was a tradeoff. Within forty-eight hours of starting the treatment I started to feel muzzy, followed by what I was told were the typical side-effects of dry mouth, dry eyes, blurred vision, dizziness and constant fatigue.

The tricyclic medication eventually left me feeling sluggish and lacking mental acuity, with a greatly reduced attention span and poor memory. I found driving my car a challenge, I started to have trouble urinating, and eventually my sex drive plummeted to an all-time low. Although sex hadn't been good for a long time, in between the bouts of deep depression I had at least tried to make a concerted effort. Essentially, despite still being very keen to make love with Jacqui, it was as if a link was now missing. As a consequence, arousal became increasingly more difficult. I was lucky if I could sustain an erection for more than a couple of minutes.

This was both embarrassing and demoralizing, and I was getting more and more confused and frustrated. After all, this was medication that was meant to be clearing up my depression and offering me new opportunities to enjoy life again on all levels. As it was, I felt I had simply been moved from one prison to another. Perhaps this course of action was offering me new opportunities, but it was not giving me the lease of hope and new life I had expected from the day I handed my prescription over the pharmacy counter. It was not an acceptable trade-off.

Six weeks into the Prothiaden I felt as if I was surrounded by a giant invisible bubble. Although I was not overweight (anything but) I felt bloated and suppressed. Mild headaches were common, restricted to small portions of my brain. There were times when I could run two fingers along the lines these headaches seemed to follow beneath my skull. I was anxious to go back and discuss this unexpected turn of events with Michael.

It seemed he had heard the story before, from many other patients. He assured me that most of these side-effects would lift, adding that it was important to drink plenty of water, take regular exercise, try to keep my mind off the negative aspects and concentrate on the positive side of my recovery. I should keep reminding myself that I was feeling more hopeful now, and that the dark clouds of depression had lifted to the point where I could get out of bed and stay out of it for longer than I had been used to doing. The truth is, it's easy to smile and hide the hurt and confusion and frustration and disillusionment, and that was precisely what I was doing now.

I wanted to discuss these side-effects with other sufferers. Not surprisingly, people were reluctant to talk about their failing sex lives; but that, of course, only thwarted me more. Maybe it *is* difficult to ask someone if they're having problems getting a hard on, but that for me was one of the great unacceptable conditions of 'taking my medicine'. As far as I was concerned, it was not the sort of life I wanted.

One man who was prepared to talk about his problems of this sort said he had gone back to his doctor to talk about alternative ways of getting well, but was told there were none. 'Either take the antidepressants or get depressed again,' he was told. When he asked about the sexual dysfunction, the doctor told him, 'It's one or the other, John. You can live without sex. It's much more difficult to live with depression.'

'I'm not depressed any more,' John told me miserably, 'but when do I get a real life?'

His words represented another crossroads in my life. After that conversation, I came to loathe the side-effects these chemical bullets were having on me. I needed to start asking when I could come off my antidepressants. Of course the drugs helped me to feel well again physically, but I was beginning to feel that they were only giving me the small picture. I wanted to see the big picture – one that filled me with feeling and depth and colour and real life, one that I had not seen for as long as I could remember. I knew now that I would settle for nothing less.

14

THE VALUE OF INTUITION

I hated having to take the Prothiaden tablets, but I also knew the consequences of not taking them. Nevertheless I refused to believe that I had to remain in this 'waiting room' frame of mind for the rest of my life. My mind was still refusing to offer me the one component I needed in order to be complete again: a positive desire to live. I didn't want to die; I simply didn't know why I wanted to live. If I couldn't find someone or something to cure me the way I wanted to feel cured, I was going to have to take charge of my own deliverance.

Like my mother, I have an enquiring mind; when my brother and sister and I were children she always encouraged us to look up things we didn't understand in the encyclopaedia which she and my father had bought us. So, now that my daily 150mg of antidepressants were taking effect and offering me a crutch of support during my waking hours, I had started to read a good deal about matters of the mind. My own mind terrified me with the relentless torture it was capable of inflicting. In past times the lion tamer came equipped with a whip and a chair; now I was going to arm myself with knowledge against my own ferocious and unpredictable beast. I was eager to learn as much as I could from other people's knowledge and experience of depression: what might have caused it, what might eventually cure it, and what effects these strange pills were having inside me while I tried to get back to a normal lifestyle.

I devoured books on psychology that seemed effort-lessly to dissect and analyse everything that could possibly go wrong with the three and a half pounds of greyish matter that sat between my ears. But many of these works that I read so voraciously didn't answer my questions, or else gave me answers that I felt weren't good enough. Much of what I read left me feeling as dizzy and confused as my condition itself. Some of the books I got hold of, written mainly by psychiatrists and psychologists, argued unceasingly that drugs and cognitive therapy respectively were the only proven 'cures' for depression. I felt like some sort of dysfunctional, half-finished reject who hadn't made the grade. But I wasn't prepared to look forward only to a dimly lit existence consisting of either a mood-altering medicated semi-retirement or, failing that (if I chose not to go down the drugs route), a continuous roller-coaster of emotional mood swings.

I checked out the net, to little avail. Apart from medical websites which merely repeated everything that various doctors had told me, and a handful of sites updated by sufferers who felt they had been given a raw deal by their doctors and psychiatrists, and urged visitors not to succumb to the drugs that had destroyed their own lives, there was little to encourage me to believe I could do much on my own to improve my condition.

Despite this apparent setback, I kept telling myself that I needed to remain hopeful, open and optimistic, and tried hard to socialize with my wife and close friends. But often it seemed like too much hard work, and I guess that when I did go out in the evenings I only put the effort in for Jacqui's sake. She would plead with me when I wanted to stay at home, telling me she knew how widows must feel in the company of couples. I knew she didn't mean it maliciously, but such comments hurt me to the core. It was easy for her to assume, because I was now firmly ensconced in the antidepressant treatment, that I must be nearly better.

Whilst agreeing with her that I was greatly improved, I knew there was this large chunk of the jigsaw still missing. She argued that I was possibly looking for too much, that I was too perfectionist, too much of a stickler for detail. If I committed myself to something, I always saw it through meticulously. *Perhaps she's right*, I thought. *Maybe I'm looking for something I can't have*. But I realize now that I had to feel that way. In order not to feel like I did, striving for that elusive quality that would redeem me and make me whole again, I would have had to stop being hopeful – and, thank God, that never happened.

Treating depression with antidepressants is simply a means of removing the blindfold that has shut out the light of living for years. They enable the brain to produce a couple of important chemicals that have been in short supply, but they cannot supply hope. What's lacking here is a vital component, an unconscious quality that makes each of us what we are as individuals: intuition.

I want to take a moment here to explain how I understand the concept of intuition. First and foremost, it should not be confused with gut instinct, which is a spontaneous reaction based on exactly what I am feeling at any given moment. My gut instinct tells me to run when a dog snarls and crouches ready to spring and attack. However, my intuition tells me to remain calm and collected, not to make any stupid moves but to back off slowly. Maybe he'll spring, maybe not, but if I follow my intuition, not my gut instinct, I have a better chance of remaining in control of the situation.

A young student recently summed up the difference very well. He told me he had been offered an Ecstasy tablet at a school disco. Most of his schoolmates knew him as a boisterous, fun person, and they watched in fascination as he made up his mind. His gut instinct told him to swallow it for the moment; his intuition, however, told him he could be dead or brain-damaged within hours of doing so. In the end, his intuition won out.

Intuition is the power of the mind to perceive the truth of things without reason or analysis. But I have to remind myself that it will only work if I am prepared to leave myself open to its far-reaching persuasive powers. Sometimes following my intuition can seem boring and contrived, like always doing the right and proper thing even though I sometimes want to be reckless and go with the crowd, or with the more exciting gut instinct. That's my prerogative. I am entitled to make that choice, and no one else can make it for me. However, if I (and you, and anyone else for that matter) want hope to play an intimate and valuable part in the direction of my life, I have to start living according to my intuition and what it is telling me *about me*. Following my own intuition, I was sure, was the path I must take to help me become a whole person again.

15

THE SILENCE THAT KILLS

Now that I had been officially diagnosed as suffering from depression, with the information on my medical records for all time, I had become part of a considerable group of people who are largely misunderstood, often shunned and frequently neglected by the 'perfectly balanced' remainder of the population, who tend to feel dirty or nervous or embarrassed in our company. I had 'the dreaded D', as I heard the wife of one sufferer describe it not long ago. Not getting the allusion (a new one on me), I jokingly remarked that I didn't understand and enquired if her husband had a problem with diarrhoea. She put me right on that one, then told me she didn't want to talk about it, that I wouldn't understand, that no one understands. Then I explained that I too had been through all this, but had survived and come out the other side. After that there was no holding her back.

For two hours she spoke to me about her husband's torment, about her silent abandonment, about their secret pact that no one outside their immediate families should ever know. But an untold story can kill: with the benefit of hindsight I know it is imperative to let the light in and to enable the talking to begin, openly and frequently, in order to encourage new growth, to develop the desire in both sufferer and partner to talk unselfconsciously about the feelings of both of them, and to realize that there are many other people out there who are going through the same traumas and feeling the same way.

Before I was diagnosed and started to get better I felt my condition's one real, unbeatable strength was its invisibility: *It's not really there so it's better left unspoken about* – and that's another way people keep it to themselves. In the first few weeks of my recovery some inbuilt mechanism seemed to be discouraging me still from telling anyone; so I didn't, and as a result I remained stifled and shut out. I was beginning to feel marginally better, but who would ever know if it all remained a dirty, despised secret?

So I discussed my feelings with Jacqui, and we agreed that we should tell our families and closest friends – tell them not that I was suffering from depression, but that I was in the process of recovering from depression. The message of 'recovering' is always a psychologically better one to give out than 'suffering'. People tend to respond more positively, even though they don't fully understand. They express a desire to help wherever possible. They tend to offer encouragement rather than run for the hills. When I told people I was at this stage I got a great lift knowing that others were aware I was on my way to getting better. Because I was now starting to have occasional feelings of well-being and peace, and was getting a little stronger each day, I really wanted to believe that my recovery had started in earnest and that I was no longer suffering from full-blown depression, even though the suffering had by no means completely gone away. I wanted my friends to know about it because I wanted to hear their questions and assuage their curiosity. I felt I should be an open book, transparent and unabashed about what I was coming through, and tell them honestly about something I was trying both to understand and to come to terms with.

My ongoing recovery was a difficult journey, but talking eased the toughness of it all. Recovery became easier because I chose to speak out, to spew out twisted feelings that were no longer scary once they had been brought out into the open. Because my mind was no longer so cluttered and shut off, my thinking started to become more productive and my feelings calmer and more beneficial to me.

The decision is mine, I would remind myself whenever I felt nervous talking about a topic that most people feel uncomfortable with. It just had to be done like this. *There is no other way*, I kept telling myself, *except to talk about it*. I could have kept it as 'our little secret', something sinister and foreboding and destructive that only my wife and my doctor and I knew about, for ever. But if that had been the decision I chose to make, I believe nothing would have changed for ever. I would have chosen to remain in the dark, to suffer in unrelieved silence. Knowing no different, people might have looked on and thought I was 'a bit odd', and I would probably still be none the wiser about this condition that had been trying to wipe me off the face of the earth and making a bloody good job of it.

Thankfully, I decided otherwise. I didn't want to spend the rest of my life suffering silently. I wanted to recover fully, and if that meant recovering publicly, which in hindsight is what I ended up doing, so be it. There is something positive and beneficial about letting people who love you know that you have suffered but that you are now recovering to the best of your ability. Standing up and announcing, 'I am getting better, thank you', sends all the right messages of encouragement and hope to the body's immune system. By sending them, we strengthen our resolve and gather resilience that carries us along this path with greater determination to go that extra mile. A problem shared is a problem halved – a truism, admittedly, but one that has never held more weight than it does in the silent, boarded up world of depression. And a problem shared frequently enough can become a problem resolved.

In the later stages of my recovery, and since that time, people have written to congratulate me on being 'brave' in 'coming out' and speaking publicly, 'fearlessly', about my own experience of depression. They tell me they wish they too could be that brave. I tell them I had no choice. I had to talk. I had to tell my story. If I hadn't, it might just have killed me.

In the very early days, though, it wasn't that easy. I often marvel when I see a small baby taking his or her first steps unaided. When I first started to announce the news that I was recovering from depression to various groups of people I was terrified. Nevertheless I always tried to do so proudly, with a smile on my face, to show just what I believed I was managing to achieve in very small baby steps; and those announcements helped me to take ever bigger steps.

Some of my friends smiled back and refused to believe

me. I had never stopped presenting my radio show, after all, even though at times I could never have done so without my marvellous producer and her colleagues, who carried me without knowing why I was so exhausted. Other friends shook my hand; one of them hugged me and told me in a whisper that he too had been prescribed antidepressants only three months before.

In quieter moments people asked me to describe my depression, to tell them what it had been like in my suicidal moments when I had been thinking about death in such a perversely positive way. I told them, among other terrible memories, about a particular night when my depression was perhaps at its worst and I might truly have killed myself had I not found empathy at the end of a telephone line. Nothing could have demonstrated better the need to be able to talk to others.

I was alone in the house that night: my wife was out with friends, my daughters staying with their grandmother. It was a Friday evening and everyone I knew was out socializing – under normal circumstances I would have been out with them. At about ten a friend called. He rang the doorbell five times, but I didn't answer it. From the kitchen, where I had been sitting in darkness for two hours, I could see his face peering in through the frosted glass door. Eventually he gave up and went.

It was Jacqui who would have found me when she returned home. I could have destroyed her life for ever that night – her ambitions, her dreams, her choices and her happiness. Indeed, she might never have recovered from the shock of finding me dead in our own home by my own hand. My three beautiful daughters would have had to carry the broken, razor-sharp memory with them wherever they went: *Our father killed himself. He kept it all to himself and shut us out of his life. He told us when we were growing up there should be no secrets between people who love each other. He told us he would die for us, but he didn't – he died for himself.*

Instead, I called the Samaritans. The man who answered was soft-spoken and gentle in his flow of simple words, drawing me into his confidence, assuring me in just a few seconds that there was nothing to be afraid of. Yet I froze, standing there in the darkness of the cool kitchen, aware now of the silence of my house, the place my wife cared for and looked after so lovingly, the place where my children proudly brought their friends to play. I tried to talk, but I couldn't. I knew I needed to. I had to get it out, to vomit out the thoughts that haunted me. I had to talk in the silence in order to hear this sweet man's voice soothing me again – or else I would hang up, and then what? Oh, Jesus!

'I'm still here,' the quiet voice coaxed. 'There's no hurry. Take as long as you want. Talk when you want to.'

And then I managed to start talking, and went on talking for almost an hour, and he listened and coaxed me a little bit more each time I hesitated. I told him living wasn't worth it, that only death would stop this horrible house of horrors that lived in my head in some place where it couldn't be reached. And then gradually, as I talked, I felt I was beginning to cleanse myself of this filthy, depressing inner darkness that made me smell like death. And I cried gently when I felt I had said as much as I could to this kind stranger.

My plea for help had become a tidal wave of confused thinking that didn't feel so overwhelming once I had spewed it out into the open that night. By the time I had finished, my one-sided conversation had become two-sided. And after I had said goodbye I felt differently. I turned on the lights around the house and banished the darkness outside me, and then switched on the heating so that the room began to feel warm. I felt at home.

And then the phone rang. My heart pounded. *Not now*, I begged. I was about to walk away, shut the door on the ringing noise and ignore it when something told me not to.

It was John from the Samaritans. He was calling to see if I felt better. He wanted to check that I was alive, that I now wanted to live. He had called not because it was his job to do so – a kind of after-sales service – but because he personally wanted me to live and to survive this awful ordeal. John saved my life that night.

Now, as I opened up about my depression to my friends, at the risk of boring them – or frightening them – I talked and talked and talked once again. Each time I expressed a little more, another episode from the silent years, and each time I smoothed my path a little more. With each of these conversations I became better and more fluent at chasing away the demons that had chased me for years, forcing them gradually back into the past out of which I was slowly stepping.

For most sufferers, however, their depression is an

untold story, one that has no beginning, no middle and no end. It's a story that lacks words, characters or genre. It doesn't fit into anything they have ever read. It's a story that most people find impossible to tell anybody, 'and even if I could,' one man once said to me, 'who'd want to listen to me anyway?' Sadly, it's often the untold story of depression, the failure to reach out for help, the inability or reluctance to tell that story – as in the sad case of my old friend Derek – that drives someone too far.

It was the ability to express my feelings and experiences, to tell my story like I knew I needed to in order to move forward, that helped me to lay the new foundations that would enable me to grow again, only this time to grow differently. Slowly but surely, day by day, I was getting stronger.

16

A STATE OF MIND

I believe that antidepressants do work, but only if they play their part in recovery alongside the need to express what we are feeling and thinking. Certainly in my case I needed to send a strong message to my immune system that every time I took a pill it was helping me to heal in the same way that I was receiving hope each time I shared my difficulties by talking about them. Recovery, healing, is a two-way circuit.

If I had told myself that these tablets were useless, that the exercise of taking my 'fix' each evening was pointless, I believe nothing would have happened – these pills would have had no effect whatsoever because the message I was sending to my immune system would have been, *What's the point? This is a waste of time.* Instead I charged up my immune system by sending it an unwavering message of steel hope. Each time I swallowed one of my little red pills I told myself, *This is an extra step on the road to feeling better still. Tomorrow morning I am going to feel even better than I do this evening.* There were days when I was tempted to question the point of this message-sending, but I blanked it, rejecting the idea of entertaining any doubts. I refused to accept anything other than optimism, hope and the future. *Keep pushing,* I kept telling myself, *and you will get better.*

By sending this message inside, every time I swallowed my prescribed amount of medication I felt I was doubling its strength and efficacy, doubling my determination to get well, doubling the efforts being made by my immune system to restore me to full health. And finally, most important of all, I felt I was doubling the prospect that I could and would recover fully in less time than most doctors would predict it might take to recover even partially.

My depression had gone on for so long unattended that it required a course of this kind of medication to enable me to give my life a sense of focus. Nevertheless I knew that antidepressants were only part of the answer and that they had unattractive side-effects; for me, they were really no more than a helpful leg-up in the greater process of recovery. And so, very soon after I started taking the tablets I wrote down the date when I would begin to wean myself off them: it was to be exactly a year from the date I commenced the course.

It's one thing to write down a date in a diary, of course, but quite another to act on it when the day comes. In fact I was quite scared at the prospect. But Michael devised a carefully phased three-month programme of withdrawal, reducing the strength and intake a little at a time. After six weeks of this regime I felt I was ready to quit altogether. The brain is a clever machine, but it can also be cleverly conned into believing that it's still getting its daily 'fix'. If the withdrawal process from mood-altering medication is done discreetly, the brain won't recognize what's happening.

Because it was all done so well, the only changes in the

way I felt were positive and beneficial. My acuity and memory started to return quickly, which seemed a little strange at first – I suppose I had grown used to the effect of the antidepressants on these areas. Everything was now starkly sharper: conversations, music, TV, pictures and even people. I tucked away my repeat prescription in a drawer for future reference if ever I wanted to remind myself of the past, which I was sure would be unlikely.

I have been talking about the brain here, not the mind: there are important differences. The brain is a physical entity within the head, a lump of yellowy-greyish spongy matter that sits between the ears under the protective 'shell' of the skull. It houses the biological motor and biochemical gearbox that keep the body running healthily and normally. It controls balance and coordination, muscle and nerve efficiency. It is the storehouse that controls the digestive, hormonal and nervous systems, the heartbeat and breathing, and many more of the auto-mechanical activities that our bodies rely on. It is the brain, not the mind, that is affected by antidepressant medication.

The mind, on the other hand, is not 'matter' in the physical sense – even though mind and brain are inseparable. In my opinion the mind is everywhere, in every single cell of my body. Indeed, each cell has its own mind, which converses and liaises with the others and listens to them – my mind never stops listening. It extends outwards to the furthest point I can see, and can be found deep inside me when I need to concentrate on something. It assists me in times of trouble and congratulates me at times of success. It is that feeling of warmth and belonging I get when I'm engaged in friendly conversation. It enables me to be reflective, sad or happy. It is on the other end of a telephone line when I am calling a friend to ask for help. It is in my awareness that something good or bad is about to happen. It is in my dreams and night-mares. It is in my reaction to an old photograph of my daughters. It has been in my moods and my personality since the time I was conceived, just as it continues to create new moods and carve out new personality traits as I grow in life.

My mind determines my emotional patterns, in the same way that my emotions determine how my mind will feel and react to such feelings. As a result of a lifetime of personal experience and interaction, my mind recognizes states such as hopelessness, loneliness, optimism and joy faster than the smallest fraction of a nanosecond – faster, some people say, than the speed of light. It associates these states with different places and people and times, and with the emotions I have come to associate with every single experience I have had in my lifetime. My mind connects me to these states based on what it remembers from similar experiences in the distant and recent past. Every feeling I have ever experienced, based on everything I have ever done, is remembered by my mind. It cannot be swapped for another mind. It cannot be detached from my person *because it is the person*. It cannot be isolated from the way I think or act. My mind is my self.

For each of us, the mind is the spiritual valve that keeps the human brain and body connected to the source of life. It is that invisible dimension that places us at the centre of our own universe. For each of us, unconsciously, that source is uniquely different. It might be God or it might be some other supernatural power. For some it might be their partners and children, for others it could be their jobs or the feeling of stepping into their neatly manicured garden after a hard day at the office. For yet others it might be the feelings they experience walking along an empty beach or through a lush green wood. Whatever, the source of life is connected to each of us through the human mind. None of us can exist without our mind, which is one of the main reasons why people who suffer from severe depression frequently feel like killing themselves.

Science might argue that this concept of the mind cannot be proved in experiments or even on paper, which is true. But I believe that in order to understand the difference between brain and mind I have to see the mind from a spiritual, supernatural point of view. Psychiatrists and scientists are often extremely reluctant to believe in the spiritual dimension of life, and to entertain the idea that an invisible force called the mind, as distinct from the brain, might influence the way we feel beyond our ability to understand just how powerful an effect it exercises over the brain and body. The mind-versus-brain argument has been written about extensively, so I won't add anything further here except to emphasize that for me depression was an emotional storm raging within something far greater than the brain inside my skull: it permeated every single aspect of my life. It was not just physical but also physiological, biological and spiritual. It invaded every molecular pinpoint in my body. It surrounded me, entering the spaces around me. It coloured my impression of the people I met, of who I was and who I was not. It beat me to everything every time. It stayed ahead of me, and lurked behind me. In short, it extended way beyond my thinking and feeling to permeate every aspect of my life.

I find it odd that doctors refer to a depressed 'state of mind', not a depressed 'state of brain', and yet continue to target the brain even though it's the mind that's screaming out for attention. Perhaps this is why anti-depressants work for some people but not for others. Perhaps reaching beyond the brain and looking for a more complete, spiritual-based human being, rather than simply addressing a chemical imbalance in a bodily organ, would enable greater attention to be focussed on the emotional, feeling aspects of depression.

Certain areas of psychology continue to emphasize that our thoughts influence our feelings. But our feelings register a million times faster than our thoughts. Surely, therefore, we don't feel because we think, we think because we feel: our feelings are what give way to our thoughts, what determine exactly what we will think. If this sounds unlikely, try gently sticking a pin into your fingertip. What is the first thing that happens? You feel pain. Only then do you think, *Ouch, that hurt!* In situations like this the feeling of pain registers before a message is sent to the brain allowing us to conceive the feeling in thought form, at which point we are able to make sense of what has actually happened to us. But if we cannot transform the sensation into thought form, fear and anxiety prevail and we are left in the dark wondering what it was all about. If this sensation continues, we quickly become depressed.

Here's another example. I am walking down the road minding my own business when I suddenly feel a sharp physical pain between my shoulder blades that propels me forward and knocks me to the ground. I can feel this intense pain but it makes no sense yet: it could be a fist, a piece of falling debris or even a heart attack, but I don't know that. My mind feels the sensation of pain, but it cannot yet send the necessary message to my brain which will enable me to rationalize this pain and its cause. It is only when I turn round and see that someone rushing past has elbowed me out of the way that my brain can put the cause of my sudden pain into thought form so that what has just happened makes sense to me.

This is a very obvious example of a situation where the mind and the brain are out of synch: they normally work together continuously, preferably in harmony, even when we are asleep or distracted by something like our favourite TV programme. It also points to the way depression can affect the connection between brain and mind. Sufferers of severe ongoing depression which remains untreated regularly talk of feeling nothing but a numbing, invisible pain, as I did myself. The normal seamless, effortless connection with the brain, which would help to rationalize that pain, is absent.

In severe depression, there is no rational thinking to tie in with much of the emotion and feeling that the sufferer is experiencing. Feelings seem to bob up out of nowhere, like balls of tumbleweed rolling up and down the main street of a deserted frontier town in a Western movie. We don't know precisely how we are going to feel in a couple of minutes' time. The brain cannot put these jumpy, hare-brained feelings into a logical, rational thought form for us to understand and deal with. It's almost as if the mind has decided that it no longer wants to play with the brain, so the latter is left sending out all sorts of random, botched thoughts, flooding the body with inappropriate chemicals and messages at the most unsuitable times, while the mind unconsciously continues to trigger all sorts of strange emotions that will affect us deeply until such time as this crucial pair are reunited and restored to their proper working relationship within our lives.

So in depression, then, feelings and emotions make no sense, because there is no logical thought pattern to what the sufferer is feeling. It is a truism that the mind has a mind all of its own – a truism that makes perfect sense to me from where I stand today, having come through a long period of painful and at times severe depression. During the early stages of my recovery, when the anti-depressants were dealing with the worst of the symptoms, it was already clear to me that it was the way I had been feeling that had been causing me to be so depressed – not the other way around.

Because many psychiatrists believe it is a chemical imbalance in the brain that causes depressed people to feel so negative and hopeless they try to rebalance areas that have shown up as flawed on brain scans, claiming that these are the areas that suffer from and even cause first depression and then malfunctions in the rest of the body. But as a former sufferer from depression, I am convinced their theories are untrue – quite the reverse, in fact. In my opinion, it is our feelings and the way we react emotionally to what is going on around us that are the chief cause of depression; for me, it is these feelings that cause the chemical imbalance in the brain that often requires medication to put it right.

I see depression, therefore, as a mood disorder, caused by an ongoing long-running crisis of the emotions, of the utterly confused way we feel at the very deepest level of our beings – our minds. And if depression doesn't start in the brain, why should psychiatrists be treating the brain with heavy-duty medication that alters moods, suppresses the ability to think and act properly and responsibly, and may ultimately impair parts of the brain that need not have been targeted in the first place?

17

COMFORT, STRETCH AND PANIC

Years ago, I came across this saying: 'If your boat doesn't come in, swim out to it.' Still on antidepressants, I knew that the energy I derived from them would be put to best use reinventing my life. And the best way to get there was to salvage what was good and positive and promising about it – those aspects and qualities I liked about myself, as distinct from those that would drive me deeper into the blackness. It was no good waiting around in the hope that someone might turn up to point me in the right direction or simply tell me what to do. What I must now do was build from the foundations up, instead of searching aimlessly for the elusive cure that we all like to believe will come along one day. The truth is that it won't 'just come': we have to set to and create something better for ourselves, by ourselves – something that is guaranteed to last.

If I was going to change my life I had to change the way my mind worked, and the only way to do that was to implement those changes at the very core. But, even though I was now equipped with an understanding of how important hope and optimism and intuition were in the greater plan, I had no idea how to go about this change of mind.

Then, one afternoon while out strolling with my father, I suddenly realized that change was not really what I was looking for. For me, to change was simply to *ex-change*, to swap one state for another – something I had been doing all my life. But I knew now that it was no good settling passively for whatever mood my mind had slipped into, and stumbling over life without thinking I had any say in what I wanted for myself. Then and there I realized I would never be content with the slight shifts and variations on the same theme which are all that such exchanges offered. I wanted something much bigger, much grander. It was time for a brand-new theme.

I can still recall the moment this frightening notion flashed across my mind. My father and I were walking in an area of Dublin's Phoenix Park called the Fifteen Acres, where Pope John Paul II had celebrated mass in 1979 before a devoted crowd of one million; it was a beautiful evening and I was watching the most breathtaking of sunsets, with fiery streaks of blood-red orange spread out across the clear sky. I had obviously sent an incredibly strong message to my unconscious mind because the euphoria and peaceful acceptance, and the reassurance that I was at long last on the right path, left me breathless with amazement.

Where had this bolt of inspiration come from? I believe it came from somewhere deep within my being, because for a very long time I had unconsciously been sending messages pleading for a new direction, for a positive sign to show me how to go about this major task of finding my true self. The answer I got back was that my true self was not 'out there' waiting to be purchased like a new car, but already being moulded within me. In order to allow this new self to shine through and come into being I had to be tough and forthright about what exactly I intended to do in order to arrive at this new beginning. I had to be prepared to let go of the old self, something which for most of us is unthinkable – but only because we don't trust our intuition to guide and direct us. Once we do the unthinkable, it is no longer unthinkable.

Allowing our intuition full rein like this is a bit like gatecrashing a private party. What is it that makes us want to gatecrash the party, full of people we don't know, in the first place? I suppose it's a desire to feel we can do something, anything, if we really want to. Or maybe it's a sense of adventure and 'what if?' that drives us to an action like this. To many people the mere notion seems crazy, but eventually we begin to see it as a bold, daring challenge, and by the time we're inside the door it all seems too easy and we begin to look forward to our next 'gatecrashing' challenge. 'What if?' is the voice of our intuition telling us that, unless we do it, we will never know what the outcome might have been. 'If your boat doesn't come in, swim out to it' became my silent mantra in the days and weeks and months that followed, until eventually I didn't even whisper it any more – it just became part of my innermost feeling and thinking.

My reinvention, I decided, needed to be carried out in three areas: physical, spiritual and nutritional. These three concepts add up to one thing: life. We exercise, we feel and respond, and we eat to sustain our bodies. If any one of these three develops a fault, the other two become 'infected' and the mind and body begin to deteriorate, even to die. On the other hand, when all three are working harmoniously together we can expect to live life as we would ideally wish to.

Some years ago a friend of mine asked me to look after his car for him while he was away on business for a couple of weeks. It was a 1966 red Aston Martin, like the one in the old James Bond movies. He insisted I should take it out on the road at least once a day, in order that the engine might 'get an outing'.

I was terrified to drive it. What if I were to crash it? What if someone else drove into the back of me? What if it were vandalized? I couldn't possibly afford to have it fixed. If anything happened to it, our friendship might suffer too. If I were just to leave it covered up in my garden he might never know. After all, he would be four thousand miles away in Chicago. But then again, I knew he would know, because he knew his Aston Martin as if it were a third arm. And if I *didn't* do as he had asked, that too would damage our friendship.

So on the second day I decided to drive it up the road, no more than half a mile, and then straight back home again. I ended up driving it for forty miles, and for the remainder of that fortnight drove it to work, drove it again in the evenings, and took it anywhere that people might see it and admire it. By the time my friend came home I had refilled it with petrol four times, washed it and polished it every third day and honestly didn't want to return it.

Throughout our lives, depending on our personalities and what we are doing, we move in and out of three zones which we may conveniently call comfort, stretch and panic. And that is exactly what I had been doing in relation to my friend's car. Imagine throwing a stone into a calm pond and watching the ripple effect spread out over the water in ever-larger circles. The circle closest to us represents the comfort zone, the area that we call our own space, within which we feel comfortable and secure and private. When we say, 'You're stepping on my toes' or 'You're invading my space', we usually mean that someone has entered our comfort zone unbidden and has no right to be there. When we close the front door in the evening and sit down to watch TV or read a book we are ensconcing ourselves in our personal, private comfort zone – a space into which we are not keen to allow anyone except perhaps our nearest and dearest.

The next circle, beyond the comfort zone, represents the stretch zone. This stands for the part of our lives in which we deal with other people, often reluctantly but usually with mutual respect. It's the part of our lives that includes our jobs, our social activities, our education and the pressures of everyday existence. When we use expressions like 'stretching myself', 'trying my patience' or 'really pushing my luck' it means we are engaged in the stretch zone. For most of us, the stretch zone is manageable as long as we are sure we will eventually be able to return to our comfort zone.

The final circle on the surface of the pond, the one we all try to keep out of our lives if at all possible, is the panic zone. This is the area where life goes out of control. Panic is contagious fear, often without any visible reason or foundation, and usually arises when we fail to rely on our intuition. It can be summed up in phrases such as, 'I completely lost my head', 'I couldn't catch my breath', 'It felt like my whole life was falling apart', 'I didn't know which way to turn', 'I just wanted the earth to open up and swallow me' or 'I always manage to hit the panic button.'

In a perfect life, these three zones remain completely under our control. In a balanced existence, in which we are content and peaceful, we are not afraid of venturing into the stretch zone and spending long periods there, because we know it's important to interact with other people in order to have a balanced outlook on life. If the comfort zone and the stretch zone are in equilibrium, the panic zone rarely affects our lives.

What have these three zones got to do with depression? Most people who become depressed have got lost somewhere between the stretch zone and the panic zone. They have lost sight of their goals in life, because their values are confused and bear no relation to what they are trying to achieve. They stretch themselves to the limit in an effort to find something, anything, that might give them peace of mind, but because they don't know precisely what they are looking for they end up living (in fact, barely surviving) in the panic zone. After too much time here, depression takes over everything. Depressed people then retreat to the comfort zone and stay there, terrified of the consequences of exertion, refusing to do anything that might stretch them or make them feel panicky in any way.

But if our boat doesn't come in we have to swim out to it, remember, and that may mean diving into uncharted waters. We have to stretch ourselves – something that depressed people avoid doing at all costs, but something that is imperative if their depression is to be defeated. If they don't, a vicious circle is set up.

I had done a lot of mental swimming in very choppy waters. There were times when it would have been easier to lie on my back and float, but if I had done so the strong, familiar current would simply have dragged me backwards, back into my old thinking and painful feelings. But that afternoon in the park, as I watched that magnificent sunset, I knew it was time to start swimming against the current and, in so doing, send a message to my mind that small changes were not enough.

In order to progress in my own recovery, therefore, I had to move out of my comfort zone and test the waters of my stretch zone. And to do that I needed new goals. Those goals became rooted in my programme of physical, nutritional and spiritual renewal. There was no point trying to repair a house that had already collapsed around me – I had to draw up new plans and start again from scratch. I needed, in effect, to take a blank sheet of paper and design something powerful and sturdy that would fulfil my needs as an individual. It was time to become the architect, rather than the architect's client.

But where to start? Emil Zatopek, a famous Czech middle-distance runner of half a century ago, once memorably said that you can't climb up to the second floor without a ladder. In other words, we should always aim for a reasonable goal, and then, once achieved, raise it; if we set our aim too high and can't fulfil it, we risk turning our enthusiasm and hunger to succeed into bitterness. This attitude represents perfectly the way I approached the next stages of my recovery from depression.

18

PHYSICAL AND MENTAL RENEWAL

Some time ago I had the pleasure of speaking to a beautiful model. On the evening I met her she was wearing no make-up, was dressed in a pair of casual jeans and a baggy pullover and had what looked like a tea-cosy on her head. She didn't look much like a catwalk model that night, but she was still quite stunning and vivacious.

During the course of our conversation she said she felt more comfortable without the trappings of cosmetics and expensive clothes that made her instantly recognizable, but she was also very aware of how awful she must look to other people when they saw her in public in such a casual state, as she put it. I was struck by her total lack of confidence and belief in her ability, despite her phenomenal success. She earned huge money for modelling assignments and personal appearances, yet looked like someone who had traded her inner contentment for the trappings of success and wealth. When I said she must often have felt like two different people she laughed and nodded.

'That's a good way of describing it. I guess if I had to choose I'd go for the make-up. I like to think I look beautiful but only when I'm made up. It gives me a feeling of confidence and power. It makes me feel good about myself.'

Most of us want to look good to other people – it's crucial for our confidence and self-esteem. When someone tells me I look great, it sends a rush of the feel-good hormones dopamine and epinephrine into my bloodstream, which in turn makes me smile and feel good about myself. The compliment is a tonic for my immune, endocrine and nervous systems. And that was exactly what I wanted back in my life at this moment: to feel as attractive and good-looking as I wanted to be. I wanted to look well, but more importantly I wanted to be pleased and impressed with how *I* felt I looked.

When you feel good about yourself mentally, others will detect this feeling and they in turn will feel good about you. And the offshoot of that is that you will feel good in their company. It's the same when it comes to looking good. If you give off an air of physical well-being other people will notice and often ask how you achieved it.

Physical attractiveness and inner contentment are a fantastic combination when it comes to making you feel good about yourself and about life in general. A healthy, physically defined, well-toned person stands out in a room full of strangers, not because he or she looks gorgeous but because they have an air of confidence, independence and individuality that sends out a very positive message: *I have taken responsibility for myself.* It is the result of rigorous personal reshaping, utter determination and conviction – the sort that delivers confidence and greater self-esteem as part of the reward for hard physical exercise. But it was not the reaction of others that drove me to become physically fit; rather, an internal, intuitive drive told me that, if I did so, I would have no problem defeating this thing called depression.

The reason, I think, is that the body and the mind are inseparable. Once you start to redefine the shape and appearance of your body, you automatically begin to make far-reaching changes on the inside. For a start, the immune system functions more efficiently. As a result the endocrine system, which is responsible for secreting important chemicals including serotonin and dopamine, responds more accurately. Consequently the nervous system behaves in a more balanced manner, because its immune partner is telling it there's no need to be on red alert all the time. And finally the digestive system works a treat, because part of getting physically fit is eating and drinking the right things.

Depression is full of contradictions. One huge hurdle that needs to be overcome is the inability to feel good about yourself. This is why physical exercise is so important. But while the depression is still in full swing you just don't have the will. I can recall a day in a particularly bad period during my own depression when a friend called, dressed in an athlete's vest and running shorts.

'I want to take you out for a two-mile jog,' he said enthusiastically as he ran on the spot on my doorstep. 'You need exercise. Let's go!'

I closed the door and went to bed. The mere notion made me hate him, made me want to throw up.

Physical exercise not only makes you feel better, it also makes you look better. It gives you a feeling of power – something that is totally lacking when you are depressed. However, embarking on any programme of physical fitness, making it your priority goal, requires a huge commitment. I knew when I set out on my own journey that committing myself to my goal was very different from how I might wish for something in the ordinary way. In terms of outcome 'I wouldn't mind trying out a bit of exercise' is a million miles from 'I *will* exercise and I *will* succeed.' If you merely wish for something you won't get it – not unless you're five years old and waiting for money from the tooth fairy. But in adult life, if you speak to your mind in terms of 'I will', then you *will* get what you want. Say it quietly and slowly to yourself a few times: *I will . . . I will . . . I will*, and see and feel the difference it makes.

Another word to avoid is 'try', which may seem positive but isn't. 'I'll try to get to the meeting on time' rarely works, because you are allowing yourself the excuse to be half an hour late. Once you exclude the word 'try' from whatever message you are sending to your mind you are faced with total commitment, and only you can guarantee that commitment.

When I was depressed, I could never feel good about any aspect of my person, never mind how I looked. It left me feeling powerless. Because I felt so awful, I told myself I looked awful. Consequently other people told me I looked awful. I believed them and felt even more awful about how awful I must have looked in their eyes (yet another of the many vicious circles associated with depression). My whole life revolved around other people's perceptions of what was happening to me, and their reactions of how awful my life was becoming.

Once I realized all this I knew I could change the way

other people saw me, provided I could change the way I saw myself. But I could only put this idea into practice, through a careful programme of exercise (described in Chapter 19), once the recovery had been kick-started with Michael's antidepressants.

I reckoned that if I could feel that I looked good, then in my mind I would also feel good about how I looked. I am six foot three inches tall, broad-shouldered and well-built now for someone who has just entered his forties. (And it has to be said that, now I have come out of the depression, I feel and act about ten years younger.) But before I took myself in hand and embarked on my exercise programme, among other steps to recovery, I weighed barely nine stone and looked, as I have already mentioned, seriously ill. My reaction to the sick, sad-looking reflection in the mirror was sending the wrong message to my mind. That message was: *He looks awful, so he has to 'think awful' because that's the way he seems to want to feel all the time*. But, as I now knew, I unconsciously cause myself to feel whatever way I want to feel. All I have to do in order to feel whatever I want to feel is, literally, to feel it. So I needed to change that message if I was ever going to change for good the way I felt.

Apart from the benefits mentioned above, what else did I get out of regular daily exercise? First, my circulation improved, which increased the overall benefits of my medication while reducing the severity and longevity of its side-effects. My immune system responded more quickly and effectively, sending me bundles of extra energy and a stronger feel-good factor. I felt less stressed, because I was burning off the surplus cortisol and adrenaline in my system – if their levels remain consistently high within the body they can cause depression. Less stress in turn leads to increased sex drive and thus helps to balance the reduction in that area caused by the antidepressants.

The psychological effects were great, too. Exercise distracted me from harmful habits I had developed, such as ruminating and worrying and fretting over the smallest things. I felt as though the space around me increased when I exercised – as though I was giving my mind more room to function comfortably. In short, I felt good about myself when I exercised – precisely what I had been wanting, but failing, to achieve for years.

Exercise is also crucial for mood regulation. Someone has to get into the cage with the lion to train him and pacify him, and usually it's the person who knows the animal best. No one – certainly no doctor or psychiatrist – knows our mind as well as we do, even though for years it may have cajoled and tricked us and caused us to feel depressed. No one can regulate our own moods and behaviour patterns as masterfully as we can ourselves. The man in the cage develops a unique programme of activities to train the lion and get the creature on his side. This is precisely what I wanted to do with my mind at this time.

The more regularly we exercise, the more regulated our moods become. A racehorse performs best when it is ridden hard and fast by a jockey who knows its physique and temperament. Similarly our bodies, once attuned to an appropriate programme of physical exercise, perform best when our sympathetic nervous system has been aroused, speeding up the heart rate and pulse, increasing the flow of blood to the muscles and brain, and triggering the release of glucose and adrenaline into the bloodstream. This heightened activity sends a message to the brain, via the immune and nervous systems, to release endorphins, substances which are often credited for producing that feeling called the 'workout high' that many people experience when they exercise on a regular basis.

Scientific research has proved that a brisk two-mile walk in pleasant surroundings, either alone or with someone you know and like, drastically reduces the symptoms of depression. If walking of this sort is continued on a daily basis indefinitely, the feelings associated with depression will eventually be displaced, leading to a more hopeful, optimistic outlook on life.

A couple of months after beginning the recovery process workout exercises are an option, either at a gym or at home. Gentle cardiovascular exercises for ten to fifteen minutes a day are good for the heart, for the circulation and for muscle development, all of which contribute to strength and confidence. Improvements to the physique will be observable in a few weeks – and to moods in mere days. The bottom line is improved body image and self-esteem.

There is more at play here than simple chemical changes within the brain and body. When exercise burns off the cortisol and adrenaline in the bloodstream it replaces them with more favourable neurotransmitters (tiny drops of chemical juice) such as dopamine and serotonin. These are like small messengers that carry 'happy' news along the information highway within the body. Regular exercise keeps the information highway squeaky clean, ready to receive messages and pass them on to the right place. Each neurotransmitter jumps between brain cells, and between cells in other organs and parts of the body, across a tiny gap called a synapse. The longer a person's behaviour is depressed, the more faulty the vital connection between these tiny gaps becomes. Eventually, once the depression has taken a firm grasp, the neurotransmitters don't work as effectively as they should, and in time may fail to work altogether.

This is why antidepressants are prescribed. It is my firm, unfailing belief that if people who are depressed were to take regular, vigorous exercise they might well not need to take antidepressant medication. Or, put another way, physical exercise, started gently and progressively accelerated to a comfortable level of exertion, as I did in my own recovery, is the one sure way to overcome depression.

19

EXERCISE AND BEYOND

Remembering Emil Zatopek's words, I didn't start my exercise programme over-ambitiously. In fact, I spent days just looking at trainers and exercise gear before ever contemplating buying! My exercise programme itself was drawn up over several months. And, as everyone should, I checked with my doctor that I was not putting myself at any sort of health risk.

I started with walking, which, as I said in Chapter 18, is a superb way to get going. I imagined it as a way for my mind to see itself moving forward into the future, where all sorts of wonderful possibilities lay for me. The great thing was that I could decide on how far 'into the future' I wanted to walk each day. It could be a short, gentle stroll on a sunny day or a tough, fast walk against a strong wind. But there was one thing I kept in mind at all times: if I was walking, I was always moving forward.

I have reached a point in my life where, if I am not happy with something, I can change it into whatever I want it to be – something that will benefit me instead of impeding me. After a few months of walking, I wanted to add workouts to my programme. I started by going to gyms, but my approach changed when I came across a book called *Beyond Built* by Bob Paris, a world-class champion bodybuilder and fitness expert, which had become a bestseller in many countries. The title alone spoke volumes to me, and I would have bought it for that reason alone.

The book explained that our bodies are structures that will age and mature and become diseased according to how we decide to treat them. What we have to start with, the status quo if you like, is the state of 'built'. Following on from that, Paris's main message was simple: if you're not happy with the way you look, change it. *Beyond Built* was telling me that I could continue to mould and change that 'built' body state as often as I liked into whatever I liked, and for as long as I wanted to. That was something I definitely liked the sound of. I wanted a new body that would instil in me a new frame of mind. Whenever I looked in the mirror I felt scrawny and lifeless and I hated what I saw, which said a lot for the way I felt. I wanted tone and definition, muscular arms and legs, a well-defined chest and broad shoulders. This felt like a tall order, but Paris's own picture on the front cover of his book left me feeling that, if he could do it, then so could I. I didn't want to win any bodybuilding competitions, but I did want a body that would help me to feel good about myself, knowing that this sense of feel-good was a message from my mind that things were looking up. This was exactly what hope meant to me: that I could look ahead with confidence and optimism, rather than always looking back with disappointment and dejection.

And then I extended the idea of Paris's basic message beyond the physical sphere and thought that, if it was possible for me to change the muscular shape of my body and redefine the way I looked physically, I must also be able to change my mind. And if I could change the way my mind worked inwardly, it seemed logical that I would also change the way I perceived life outwardly.

What Paris was advocating was a proven, physically demanding twelve-week programme of tough exercises at progessively increasing levels of difficulty that would result in a 'new body'. With *Beyond Built* as my guide, I decided to stop working out at a gym. Most of the ones I had tried were impersonal, noisy places where people went not to work out but to watch and chat and pass the time in a pretty unconstructive way. By the time I had parked, changed, worked out, showered and driven home I had used up the best part of two hours, which I believed could be better spent working out at home. So I bought some relatively inexpensive weights and a bench press and set about constructing my desired physique.

I started out doing fifteen minutes every second day with some light weights – not over-exerting myself, taking care to stop when I felt dizzy or when my heart beat too hard for comfort. Within a couple of weeks, subject to huge determination on certain days, I was starting to look and feel very different. My arms and chest were becoming more defined. My body in general was looking and feeling more toned, and I was feeling better than I had ever felt in my life. I had bundles of energy, slept like a baby and was in a more lithe, nimble state of mind – a state where I could concentrate, think better and with a sharper edge than previously, and dwell less on the past and more on the future. Each 'maybe' and 'maybe not' was rapidly becoming a 'will be'. My focus was sharper. My positivity started to soar. My determination was becoming almost ruthless. There was going to be no settling for second best any more.

The reason I achieved this great result so quickly was, I believe, because I had made a pact with my mind to include it in every workout, walk and session of physical exercise. The exercise programme was paying off for me because my mind was putting down new layers of positive emotion and productive feelings, replacing the negativity which I had allowed to dominate my life for more years than I care to remember.

When we exercise, the mind is functioning at its peak. This is the time to send it positive images and optimistic messages, because it is exposed to whatever we want to instruct it to do. Working out, brisk walking and aerobics are all, if you like, forms of active meditation. We shut out the world for a time so that we can spend that time concentrating on improving ourselves. It is a mind-building opportunity as well as a physically rewarding exercise.

The times when we are engaged in physical exercise are perfect for giving ourselves a psychological boost. We all talk to ourselves, even if we do so silently. Unfortunately, most of this self-talk is negative and destructive: we analyse our thinking, interminably poring over our feelings and thoughts usually in a very self-defeating way. For most of us, self-talk is simply a stick to beat ourselves with, particularly if we suffer from low self-esteem and lack of confidence, and it can start very early in life. But, believe it or not, the negativity of this self-talk is very easy to change, and while we are exercising we have the opportunity.

When we work out, do aerobics or walk briskly, we

alter our state of mind: we offline the critical conscious mind, and tap into something much deeper with greater impact. Exercise is a form of active meditation in which we shut out the world for a while so that we can spend that time more valuably, concentrating on improving ourselves. So, because this is the time when the mind is functioning at its peak and receptive to whatever we want to instruct it to do, it is the best time to send it positive images and optimistic messages. With each exercise movement we should picture ourselves well and hopeful – as well and hopeful as we would like to be, as we *will* be. The messages are often referred to as affirmations, and we can think them, speak them, sing them or chant them – whatever we feel comfortable with – and imagine them taking root in the deepest core of our mind. Here are a few examples: 'I will succeed', 'I will be the best', 'I can be whatever I want to be – and I will.' It is also vital to feel these affirmations as well as to articulate them. Feeling them enables us to send a stronger, more penetrating message with longer-lasting, further-reaching implications.

I chose to work out in front of a long mirror, and I had two reasons for doing so. First, it is important to concentrate on the task in hand, and I knew that if I couldn't see the parts of my body which I was exercising, and witness the rapid and rewarding changes as they were taking place, my mind would be distracted. Second, I felt I had to be able to see my eyes and watch myself quietly mouthing my positive messages. I always avoided negative words such as 'not' or 'never', preferring positive ones such as 'will' and 'can' as in the examples above.

Now, a few years on, I exercise most mornings, five days a week, for thirty minutes – no more, no less. I pick a time when the house is empty, leave the phone off the hook or switch on the answering machine, and imagine that I am hanging a 'Do Not Disturb' notice on the front door. Each day I choose a different area of my body to exercise: shoulders and arms one day, legs another, chest the next, then tummy, and so on. That way I give the previous day's selected body area time to rest; most muscular growth takes place not when we are exercising, but when we are letting the relevant part of the body rest after exercising it. Every few days I allow myself a day off. Consistency is everything – there is no place for complacency. I have to be ruthless with myself in order to make the programme work. As Irish soccer hero Roy Keane once notably said, 'Fail to prepare, then prepare to fail.'

I have reached a level of feeling and experience that I want to remain at, or even develop beyond. This requires an ongoing commitment on my part, but at the end of the day I know it's always going to be well worth it. My family and close friends tell me I have never looked so well, and certainly I feel better now than I ever have in the past. But the big result is that all the feelings I experience as a result of the hard work are positive and filled with hope. None of this would have been possible or even worth while if I had not been able to reconnect with an equally crucial aspect of my life, spiritual renewal. And that was the outcome I longed for when I set myself the task of recovering.

20

My daughter Katie said to me recently, when I told her she looked and sounded too unwell to go to school, 'Dad, I'm too busy to be sick!' Within an hour she looked well again and seemed to be back to her usual bubbly self. *Too busy to be sick*, I thought. That is exactly the kind of awareness the immune system thrives on. When we are just ourselves, and not depressed, the immune system works like a well-run bus timetable, coordinating hundreds of precisely timed responses so that the body can overcome the desire to collapse – as in Katie's case. However, once we submit to empty helplessness and throw in the towel, this chain of precisely timed immune responses malfunctions. Why does it work so smoothly under normal conditions? Because we look beyond the problem, and leave the problem itself to the sophisticated system that has been put in place specifically to deal with such physiological skirmishes.

So what exactly is this immune system that I am talking about here, and have mentioned in passing on a few earlier occasions? It consists of the spleen, the bone marrow, the lymph nodes and various kinds of white blood cells, some of which circulate throughout the body whilst others reside in body tissue, including the skin. Its function is to protect us from invasion by infection: not just commonplace infections such as colds and flu, but also premature aging, degenerative ailments such as arthritis, and many other more clandestine conditions including depression and stress-related illnesses such as heart disease. If our immune system took its eye off the road for a split second, our bodies would be so badly ravaged by every conceivable virus and infection known to us (and doubtless some we have not yet heard of) that we would die a slow, cruel death.

AIDS is the classic modern example of a virus that plays hide-and-seek with the human immune system. By the time scientists have recognized and identified one particular strain, it has mutated twenty times over. The AIDS sufferer's immune system literally collapses over a prolonged period of time. People who are HIV-positive, suffering from the precursor to AIDS, are taught that they must remain unstressed and 100 per cent positive and hopeful at all times if they want to continue to lead as healthy and happy a life as possible. HIV thrives on negativity and pessimism and hopelessness because these factors cause the immune system to become uncontrollably stressed and slackened, to such an extent that it can no longer thwart the steady march of the virus.

As it is with HIV, so it is with depression. Our immune system is an information network so refined and specialized that it cannot be ignored when we are searching for a way to avoid becoming depressed, or to recover from depression.

One of the key properties of the immune system is that its cells move. Unlike brain cells, immune system cells work by 'swimming' throughout the body to wherever they are required to mount an offensive against an incoming infection, to heal a wound or to soothe pain. In recent years scientists have discovered that immune system cells make, store and secrete the neuropeptides that were previously believed to be manufactured and retained only within the brain. In other words, the immune system's cells all over the body are manufacturing the same 'information' chemicals that we regard as being mood-controllers orchestrated by the brain. Essentially, then, in some respects our immune system is capable of doing exactly the same job as the brain. Our immune system can cause our mood, or emotions, to change in a sort of two-way communication with the brain.

Hunger is one example of how the two body systems share similar functions. There is a neuropeptide called CCK which governs hunger and the sense of fullness. If we were given repeated injections of CCK we would not want to eat, no matter how long it was since our last meal. Scientists have now proved that the spleen – the 'brain' of the immune system – also contains receptors (receivers and senders of messages) for CCK. When we have eaten enough, CCK sends out a message to the brain to that effect. It is now believed that CCK receptors are present in the immune system in order to send out a signal to that system to slow down while digestion takes place.

This is interesting given that one of the symptoms of depression is loss of appetite. When our mood sinks, the production of certain important neurotransmitters and neuropeptides goes haywire. Our immune system, then, thinks like the brain, works and functions like a sub-brain and is capable of changing our moods and emotional responses. It seems logical that when we are 'just ourselves' the immune system, like its brain associate, runs like clockwork. Therefore the contrary is probably also true: if we submit to emptiness, helplessness and fear, the chain of precisely timed immune system responses goes wrong too. The choice lies with us. Our immune system, it has been proven, waits to hear our ultimate decision – a decision that can only be made by each individual.

Our intuition, which I talked about in Chapter 14, is so closely tied into an effective, finely tuned immune system that it is often difficult to distingush between immune and intuitive. The immune system is the cleverest, most intricately designed system of control and management in the world. If we were to send out only positive messages to our immune system, I believe we would never become ill. Conversely, if we *think* unwell for long enough, we will eventually *become* unwell. And one of the best ways of supporting the immune system and ensuring that it thrives is, as I explained earlier, to keep the body fit and well exercised.

21

SPIRITUAL RENEWAL

One of the key areas of my recovery involved spiritual renewal. I would even say that my recovery to date could not have been anything like as effective without the journey I undertook to find out what lay beyond the power of my healing – in other words, what it was that gave me the strength to get well again, and in doing so to build the life that has made me so happy.

The inability to be happy is probably the single most important aspect of depression that people who have never suffered have trouble understanding. Most people I know are almost automatically connected to sources of happiness that trigger themselves at appropriate moments – but depression destroys all that. One dictionary definition of happiness is 'expressing contentment, well-being and pleasure'. 'Expression', of course, is a word that takes flight and disappears when we feel depressed. I know that, in the days of my own depression, I was quite unable to express anything. In order to express things clearly I needed to connect with the one true feeling that was appropriate to whatever it was I wanted to express. But feeling was something I just could not do.

A friend who loves her garden adores the feeling she experiences on a beautiful warm day when she runs her fingers through the cool earth. She says it connects her to something that raises her spirits and makes her so joyful and content that she doesn't want the moment to end. It takes her to 'a different place'.

'Where is that place?' I once asked her.

'It's a place where the past and the future no longer matter,' she replied, 'and that feeling of the *now* takes over and becomes magnified and welcomes me in and holds on to me lovingly.' I thought it was one of the most beautiful descriptions of contentment and joy that I had ever heard. It is her ability to express her true feelings that makes her feel joyful and content, not the other way around. Her expression is her spirit – her spiritual strength, so to speak. It is the strength that opens the door to joyfulness and contentment, and therefore to hope and the feeling of belonging.

It is this loss of the ability to express our deepest feelings when and where we need to that causes depressed people, such as I once was, to become so utterly lost in their depression. Often this inability to express ourselves deepens an already dark period of bleakness and hopelessness. The feelings are all working away inside, like a pressure cooker, but we don't have either the words or the spiritual strength to express them. So initially they simmer away, waiting to release themselves through normal expression, until, thwarted, they eventually boil over, resulting in anger and self-loathing.

Scientists say there is a rational explanation: they have tracked the precise pathways in the brain along which the neurotransmitters travel with their messages that help us to express our feelings and convert them into thought power so that we can put them into appropriate words.

One of these powerful chemical messengers is dopamine. Depression weakens the production plant that oversees the availability of both serotonin and dopamine. This in turn affects an area in the brain consisting of a large group of nerves called the involuntary motor system. These nerves influence automatic functions like blinking and facial expression and posture, which explains why people who are depressed look expressionless.

While we remain expressionless we are spiritually empty, lost for words, detached from the ability to create a feeling of happiness and contentment. One man who was on his way to recovery told me that during his darkest days there was no upside for him, just a magnified downside. I knew exactly what he meant but still asked him to explain it, so that the power and facility of expression would become reinforced in his life, strengthening the spiritual ammunition that helped him, as it does all of us, to express his feelings. He told me that during the moments when he would formerly have felt happy and bright and optimistic, when he should have smiled and felt that familiar wave of pleasure and contentment sweep through him, he always felt worse than he had done before the opportunity to feel good came along. This is a classic sign of deepening depression. But as long as our lives are filled with spirit, with the energy that comes from self-expression and the ability to emit an understanding of the way we are feeling, there can be no state of depression because there is simply no room for it.

Depression is like a squatter. It can only enter when the house lies empty and unattended. I always think a happy house is filled with spirit and a life of its own. Once that spirit is evicted, for whatever reason, that 'life of its own' departs too. But not necessarily for ever – it is always waiting for an invitation to return.

If my life is spiritually well balanced and, more importantly, tuned into the greater strength that motivates me unconsciously, I don't even have to check on how fulfilling and contented and joyful my life is. I just know it is. But if I become detached from the spirit that breathes life into simple things I become chaotically confused. My feelings melt down into fear and anger and self-loathing, the three emotions that tell me my life is dangerously out of control.

So what constitutes spirituality? I don't mean going to church services or being a member of a conventional religion, although many people say that prayer has helped them greatly in healing their depression. What I mean by the term 'spirituality', and having a spiritual dimension in our lives, is experiencing the joy of creativity and curiosity.

When I was suffering from depression I got a sense of release, of expression, from writing novels. The area of the brain that deals with spoken expression is different from the one that is concerned with written expression. Written expression is richer and more rewarding because it requires greater effort to express ourselves more clearly. It allows us to retain the emotions attached to the words. A poet cannot compose while speaking aloud; a novelist cannot write a love story, or even a thriller, if he is sitting talking to a friend. Writing is the short cut to emotional expression.

An actor needs to learn his lines before he eventually,

painstakingly, becomes the character he is going to portray. Often his rehearsals will confuse and confound him, until the opening night when suddenly the real emotion pours forth and he sheds tears when he realizes that he is now the character he has been learning to express. This is spirituality, the spiritual dimension without which our lives are incomplete – the invisible and essential sixth sense we require if we are going to heal this experience of depression.

But if you are recovering from depression you will not be able to renew the spiritual aspects of your life by relying solely on antidepressant medication. Spirit, like the human mind, is not mechanical, nor is it tangible like the brain or the nervous system or the organs within our bodies. Its counterpart in the body is the immune system, which to the human eye does not exist physically. Spirit is a supernatural power that is fuelled by our feelings and emotions, our thoughts and decisions, and by the simple things we undertake every day. When we express ourselves we are talking to the body's immune system and to the mind, and in so doing we are sending the messages that nurture and nourish our spirit.

When someone tells me they don't believe in God, or in a power of some loving, benevolent type, that person is not living in a contented, expressively hopeful way. By refusing to accept that there just might be something bigger out there that just might be responsible for life's simple beauties and magic moments, this person has closed down the connection between their physical existence and a spiritual dimension that connects them both to an ability to express their feelings and emotions, and

to a belief that their mind and their immune system –
their spirit – are something more than a useful tool they
can turn to in order to dig themselves out of problems.
I'm not saying that people who don't believe in something greater than themselves are depressed. However, if
they do get struck by depression it's often more difficult,
sometimes impossible, for them to heal it if they don't
believe that a spiritual dimension is crucial in their lives,
not just to help them move beyond the problem, but also
in the connection between the spirit and the workings of
the human mind and the immune system.

When spirit increases our ability to express feelings,
the neurotransmitter dopamine flows through our system, giving us a feeling of well-being and contentment.
This brings me to another of the many problems associated with taking antidepressants. They increase the
production of serotonin in the brain, and the brain
always attempts to compensate for the physical and
chemical effects of any manmade drug introduced into
the body. So the surge in serotonin resulting from the
antidepressant results in depleted production of dopamine, since in their natural state the two are produced in
equal proportions. The symptoms of depression are lifted
by serotonin, true, but without dopamine there can be no
joy, no ability to express our feelings.

I believe that long-term reliance on antidepressant
medication robs us of the opportunity to allow the
spiritual dimension of our lives to take control again.
If we cannot heal the depressed state we are experiencing
at the very core of the human mind, the engine of this
amazing machine we call the body, then the brain can

never expect to be properly, naturally balanced again. This is the depth of the spiritual dimension that, sadly, many members of the medical profession tend to ridicule when it comes to 'curing' depression. The answer, surely, lies not in textbooks but in our ability to express the ways in which we feel, in the messages our spirit is sending us according to the ways it is causing us to feel.

There is a close inter-relationship between spirit and physical exercise, for physical exercise enables us to express our feelings. It's as if the exertion helps us to break down the great wall that separates us from the ways we would like to be able to feel. How often have you found yourself able to sort out a problem by going for a jog or taking a brisk walk? How many times have you left the gym feeling you could take on the world? That's because the determination we have felt in driving ourselves hard physically has sent a message to our innermost being, allowing the spirit to express itself and releasing a gentle trickle of dopamine into the bloodstream. This in turn sparks off an expression of healthy vibes within the immune system, which forwards the 'pleasure' message throughout the nervous system. We come away from our exercise feeling fresh, relaxed and ready for whatever the world might throw at us.

Whilst this is a physical sensation, it's also a spiritual statement. Undertaking a programme of physical exercise and renewal sends a message to the deepest part of our being: *Give me the strength I need to live the life I know I want but am having difficulty finding right now.* By sending this message home while we are busy exercising, we are planting the seed of spiritual re-edification.

This seed, if repeatedly replanted, will grow into a whole new dimension that will reshape our lives and guide us in the direction we have been searching for, perhaps down the path we have been too afraid to walk along.

Exercise is not the only way to feel what I call the 'spirit of life'. Listening to nothing is something I like to make time for every day of my life. This might sound like a very strange concept – indeed, most people believe it's impossible to listen to nothing. It's not – in fact it can turn into the easiest and most beneficial few moments of your day. Just like positive self-talk, it is an immensely empowering recharging exercise.

I choose a quiet place where I know I won't be disturbed for fifteen minutes or so – perhaps a quiet corner of the garden or in front of a beautiful picture. I select some small element of the scene before me and sit down in front of it. Then I lie back in a chair, or on a blanket, and just watch, breathing slowly, emptying my mind of unwanted thoughts and worries. I imagine I'm listening for something, like the sound of a plane or the whistle of the wind. If I'm looking at a flower bed, I look beyond the colours into the heart of the plants. If I'm looking at a picture, I look beyond it to imagine what the original scene might have been like. If I'm looking at a blue sky, I look beyond the blue for something much deeper. By looking beyond what is immediately visible, and listening quietly, it is possible to bring it to life.

What I am doing here (and there are endless varia-tions) is tapping into the deepest part of my unconscious mind and giving free rein to the spiritual energy that gives me the ability to express my deepest feelings. By allowing it to come to the fore, to guide me and to do my feeling and thinking just for fifteen minutes at a time, I have added to my life the dimension that enables me to feel joy and contentment and, most important of all, hope.

I have described my own spiritual journey here because that was my personal experience. But what was good for me might not make sense to other people. Spiritual renewal and restrengthening cannot be done alone. Although most of the 'silent' exercises I undertook can be done in private, real spiritual reinforcement can only come from aligning ourselves with other like-minded individuals who want the same things from life that we are seeking ourselves. And if we leave our lives open to these valuable individuals, they will come.

My journey started because I was ready to create a new structure, to plan the outline of the life I wanted to live, and not the life other people expected me to live. I opened my heart and spirit to the healing forces both within me and around me. I already knew unconsciously that I had what was needed right there inside me. I just needed to be shown it – and I was.

22

WE ARE WHAT WE EAT

If we don't eat or drink anything over a prolonged yet relatively short period of time we will die – no one would deny that. It follows, therefore, that the quality and quantity of what we eat and drink will also play an important part in determining both how we live and how long we live. The word 'diet' in this context has absolutely nothing to do with losing weight or slimming down. We should regard it more as a planned or prescribed schedule for living. The effects, if we don't get it right, will be felt right across the board, in our physical, mental and emotional selves.

Many of the physical effects of eating the wrong food, too little or too much are easily visible and we know what has caused our spots, overweight or bad teeth. The effects on our emotions, which are governed by what we eat and how regularly we do so, are perhaps less obvious at first glance, and certainly we are less ready to attribute them to diet. If we get too hungry, we grow angry and frustrated. If we eat too much, we become lethargic and confused. And if we eat too much processed junk food our emotions become muddled and disconnected, causing dangerous mood swings. Put simply, a bad diet will only worsen the symptoms of depression. What I ate and drank certainly contributed to my own state of depression down through the years.

Thousands of books have been written on the foods we should and shouldn't eat, and I don't propose to add to them. I am neither a dietician nor a nutritionist, but I do believe that intuitively I know more about what's good and what's bad for me than many professionals who have gleaned their knowledge from study rather than from real-life personal experience. What I want to do here is offer some general advice on what is good in terms of nutrition for the body and mind, based on the diet which I made a part of my life when I started on my recovery from depression, and which I still stick to faithfully today.

My attempt to find the perfect diet for myself – one that would supply healthy contentment and inner well-being – came about mainly through trial and error. Because I had now decided to make myself the architect of my own destiny I had to go in for experimentation in various fields: nothing dangerous, of course, but I approached things with an air of curiosity and a sense of adventure as I moved towards creating the life that until now had eluded me. Once that becomes a possibility, almost within reach, it's the perfect time to find out what each of us as an individual needs to eat and drink, in order to ensure that the duality of the spiritual journey and the physical exercise plan can make the greatest impact and continue to do so for as long as we want it to. Once we decide to take responsibility, to write our own script, we must trust in ourselves. And so now I experimented with different aspects of dietary requirements, taking on board what worked for me and ignoring those foods and drinks that didn't appeal to me for whatever reason. In diet, as in other aspects of my life, I was following the kind of intuition I talked about in Chapter 14.

Many people who have talked to me about their own depression, during and since my recovery, fell into the fast food trap way back and stayed there. A brief list of what they typically ate and drank between getting up and bedtime will give you the picture. For breakfast they had cereal, toast made from processed bread with something like chocolate spread on top, and coffee. By lunchtime they had eaten crisps, doughnuts and anything else that would stop their energy flagging. They struggled through the afternoon with more coffee, starchy snacks, soft drinks and chocolate biscuits. Dinner-time featured chips and burgers, or white rice or pasta, but rarely a fish dish and maybe only a small amount of unprocessed meat or chicken. Mid-evening saw cheese and crackers or ice cream appear, or another bowlful of cereal with full-fat milk and a dessertspoon of sugar. Not all these foods are bad, of course, but there's no balance there and lots of things that should belong in the diet are missing or in short supply. It's the sort of diet that leads to heart disease, cancer, immune system impairment and hormonal problems, let alone depression.

For years I too had eaten crap because it was convenient. Pizza, burgers and chips, hot curries and chili con carne were the order of the day. A good old traditional Irish fry-up first thing on a Saturday morning after a night of pints at the pub went down a treat. I was a stranger to fruit, and often headed off to the local Chinese takeaway of an evening. Everything seemed to be eaten on the go. Meals became like a quick pit-stop on the forecourt of the local petrol station – fill up the tank and speed off again. Proper meals at proper mealtimes were inconvenient intrusions into the day, getting in the way of more important things. It was handier to eat a slice of pizza or a starchy sandwich while I read the newspaper or talked on the telephone. Never mind fast food – most times I couldn't eat the food fast enough, and as a result much of it got left behind. Jacqui cooked proper meals at home, but I was rarely in the mood to eat them. I found the chitchat at the dinner table difficult because I felt so low, or else the alcohol would have taken the edge off my appetite and I went to bed without eating anything, either fast or wholesome.

Slowly but surely I was killing myself, filling my body with toxic rubbish that was playing havoc with my immune system. I found it hard to sleep and felt sluggish in the mornings, yet rarely had breakfast before eleven. I got cold after cold and was always hit hard by flu every January. My back ached, my shoulders hurt and I developed a classic beer belly – a gut so swollen and distended that it embarrassed me. I had turned myself into a physical wreck and, typically, I ate and drank more to console myself. Comfort eating filled the time as I waited in traffic jams, consuming sugar-laden soft drinks, chocolate doughnuts and bag after bag of sweets. Addicted as I was to junk food, I had become a walking E-loaded time bomb.

Of course, people who are depressed go in for comfort eating because sugary foods light up the brain's pleasure pathways. We crave sweet food and drink because our levels of dopamine and serotonin, and of other endorphins responsible for helping us to feel exhilarated, are very low. The carbohydrates we feel we need in processed, additive-loaded foods help the body to absorb a substance called tryptophan, which is the main building block in the production of mood-improving serotonin. We may not understand this physiological process, but we can subconsciously relate cause and effect, sugary intake and feel-good factor, and keep the process going. Within a couple of hours of that fizzy drink or iced bun, of course, our blood sugar level drops rapidly again and we are left feeling drained and sluggish, as though we are wearing damp clothes. That's when we need another fix, another bun or bar of chocolate, to get another sugar high. And so on and so on.

A further reason behind such eating habits is that, perversely, antidepressants often increase our cravings for the very foods that will reduce their effectiveness. They can trick the brain into believing that it needs more of these sugary foods and drinks, when in fact the mind is calling out for a well-balanced diet with plenty of protein, fruit and vegetables. Eating rubbish while taking antidepressant medication will only make its side-effects more severe and longer-lasting. Toxic food (which is what it is) quickly depletes the body's store of vitamins and minerals, leaving us feeling more depressed and holding up the process of healing.

Research is now beginning to endorse the theory that depression often vanishes when sugar and caffeine are removed from the diet altogether. The more of these substances we eat, the more likely that our diet is low in essential vitamins and minerals.

All I started to do when I set out to become well and healthy was to pick the right foods – those that would recharge my immune batteries and give me a more consistent energy high that would enhance my quality of life by making me feel well in myself. My physical exercise programme only worked because I was eating the right foods. The combination of physical exercise and good diet gave me the spiritual strength and upbeat well-being that I had craved for years – and that, however long it had taken me to get there, was a craving worth satisfying.

On one level food is a medicine. If someone told us that what we proposed to sit down to at dinnertime this evening would be laced with poisonous chemicals that can cause cancer cells to grow in our bodies, chances are we would skip the meal and go for a walk instead. That may sound like an exaggeration, but in many cases it's true. Most of us choose not to bother to check the covert ingredients in the foods we eat and cook for our families. Even if we did, further effort would be required to find out the potential effects on our health.

The best foods are as nature intended them to be, not messed about and tampered with by human intervention. My own recovery was undoubtedly aided by eating foods that were low in refined flour, processed sugar and artificial ingredients, and high in fibre, whole grains and natural nutrients. This kind of food will quickly restore the body's nutrient levels, increasing the natural production of minerals and restoring the all-important body–mind balance. Once that stage has been reached, depression departs.

Water is vital: drinking plenty of it keeps the body consistently hydrated, which means that the digestive system is kept purged and the immune tracts purified. I found, as everyone does, that once I started on my exercise programme I was automatically drawn to drink more water because I perspired more. Even before that time it helped me to avoid the dry mouth, fatigue, dizziness and light-headedness associated with anti-depressants. Three litres a day might sound a lot, but that's what I drink and it makes me feel energetic and invigorated. Drinking most of this quantity in the early part of the day helps to keep my energy levels high and avoids too many trips to the bathroom in the wee small hours. Water also, of course, fills up the space that might otherwise be taken by coffee, caffeine-rich and addictive, to which people with depression are nearly always drawn.

Apart from choosing the right kind of food, I found that eating little and often – four or more small meals a day rather than three large ones – helped me to achieve a kind of inner equilibrium and avoid highs and lows. Mid-morning and mid-afternoon is a good time to fill the gap with fruit, and helps to ensure I get my five-a-day, which is the recommended amount. Most fruit is fine raw, but I have also trained myself to eat some vegetables raw, which preserves the nutrients. The more we cook most fruit and vegetables, the less point there is in eating them.

The basics of my own daily diet are simple – anyone could work out a plan like this, adapted to accommodate their own lifestyle and working day, their likes and dislikes. I get up shortly after six and have a slice of wholemeal bread and a cup of coffee (yes, we don't have to cut these things out altogether!). Before I have break-fast, around ten and usually consisting of a light cereal such as shredded wheat or muesli, I will have done half an hour of exercise. Lunch, a generous helping of home-prepared chicken salad which I take to work with me, I divide into two portions so I don't eat it all at once. Fruit, as I mentioned above, fills the gap and makes a much healthier snack than the biscuits, crisps and chocolate bars I used to consume. Dinner at home is based on fish or meat, preferably grilled or baked so that there's not too much fat in attendance.

Finally, I feel it is important to believe in what I eat. I constantly tell my immune system that I know it will become even more effective in protecting me against infection because of the nutrition I am serving up to it. When I eat a hearty but healthy meal I let my mind settle on the feeling that I am rewarding my body. These quiet messages have paid huge dividends in all areas of my life, as they do in the life of anyone who decides to change their dietary lifestyle in the way I have outlined.

But does food supply all the nutrients we need? Many people think not, and feel they need dietary supplements. I first went down this route at the time when I had been taking antidepressants for a few months, and had just started my physical exercise programme at home. The exercise hadn't kicked in yet, so my mood was still low, my mind sluggish. Time would tell, I thought, if I was on the right road, but in the meantime I definitely needed something to jump-start my physical well-being. So I thought I would check out what was available and went to a local health food store. I stared at the shelves packed with brightly coloured plastic bottles and jars, many of them with unfamiliar names containing long, unpronounceable words. One of the staff was watching me and in the end I walked out, embarrassed that she might think I was intent on shoplifting. But five minutes later I was back, determined to find something that morning that I could start taking straightaway to make me feel better sooner. I was sending the right messages to my mind, and my intuition had sent me back to the shop. *It's going to be all right*, I told myself.

I don't propose to go through here all the supplements that manufacturers recommend as a 'natural cure' for depression. Apart from the fact that more research needs to be carried out into the unproven long-term effects, both good and bad, of these remedies, to describe each one would take up a whole book. Of the huge number of supplements I have tried over the years, I shall briefly describe just those that helped in my recovery. As with diet in general, there are already plenty of books on the subject to supply greater detail. It's worth emphasizing, however, that just because I believe certain supplements and remedies worked for me they may not be the definitive turning point on everyone's road to happiness and joy. They only worked for me because I had an indestructible belief in my own powers of recovery and healing at this time. I just knew I was going to get well. There were times when I didn't know how this wellness was going to come about, but my intuition told me it would. If you don't believe you are going to feel better, then absolutely nothing that you take will make you feel better. And finally there's one other important thing to remember: supplements (and, indeed, medication) will only work if used in conjunction with the overall programme which worked for me, and which I have been advocating throughout this book.

Fish oils rich in Omega-3 fatty acids are my number one recommendation to anyone. I cannot speak highly enough about the importance of incorporating them into a well-balanced daily diet – so much so that I believe they should be given to every child as soon as he or she can hold a spoon. Omega-3 fatty acids are vital nutrients that control energy production within every cell in the body. They also convert into messenger molecules, carrying important information that is crucial to a large number of body functions. A further role is to act as basic building blocks for the smooth, oily membrane that coats every cell in the body and keeps it healthy. Unfortunately these substances, along with their partner, Omega-6, vitamin C, calcium and certain other essential nutrients, are not produced by the body and so must be taken in through food (typically, for Omega-3, oily fish such as salmon, herrings and mackerel) or supplements.

We are born with an inbuilt supply of both Omega-3 and Omega-6, which depletes over our lifetime. But modern food is usually low in Omega-3 (though adequate in Omega-6) and it is therefore difficult to make up this deficiency. Depending on the levels of Omega-3 that their mother possessed while they were in the womb, babies can enter the world with either a strong or a badly depleted supply of this substance. Research shows that babies are now being born with inadequate levels because their parents and grandparents did not absorb enough of these 'caretaker' fish oils in their formative years. Children deprived of Omega-3 often find it difficult to pay attention, for instance in school, and to control outbursts of impulsive behaviour. They may also be at higher risk of depression. Teenagers and adults with a depleted supply may be more prone to hostility, violence and depression, whilst older people run a greater risk of stroke, dementia, memory loss and, as ever, depression. It has also been proved that people of any age whose levels of Omega-3 drop below a certain level may be candidates for Bipolar Disorder (manic depression) and other psychiatric problems. Plenty of good reasons, then, for adding this easily obtainable supplement to our daily diet.

Vitamin and mineral supplements can be useful, too, although the popular multivitamins are designed on the basis that we all have similar requirements, which clearly can't be true. Each of us is unique in terms of gender, age, state of health, physiology, brain function, lifestyle, outlook and so on. I opted, therefore, for a selection of solo vitamins in a kind of bespoke package tailor-made for my own personal requirements, and I found the best place to get answers was a good health food shop whose staff had reputable qualifications. Brands, prices and dosages can all be bewildering and I feel it is always much better to seek professional advice than to buy in ignorance. These people will know best about the vitamins and minerals that can specifically affect depression, healing or exacerbating it depending on our intake of them, and will point the otherwise confused buyer to the right product or products.

23

RENEWING VALUES AND BELIEFS

Hope has been a central theme throughout this book. It was the driving force behind my recovery once I had managed to get my foot on the first rung of the ladder, and it continues to be the most crucial component in what motivates me in my life today. Hope sustains each one of us, creating the momentum which we turn into outcomes that we strive to achieve.

I believe there are two forms of hope: active hope and passive hope. In his book entitled *Hope*, Dr Arnold Hutschnecker describes active hope as 'the inner mental force that triggers the human will into action'. Active hope is directly connected to my happiness and my contentment. It gives me the strength to overcome the obstacles that life throws in my way, from something as straightforward as getting out of bed in the morning to something as complex as passing my driving test. It helps me to stay on course, fulfil my goals and commitments, and achieve the outcomes I set for myself.

But if my existence is bogged down in a state of passive hope – which is really hopelessness, no hope at all – nothing is achievable, not even getting out of bed. Stuck in this miserable state I can expect to suffer from depression, stagnate and eventually die. This state of passive hope exactly characterizes the way I had lived for years –

resorting to a kind of fantasy escapism in order to distance myself from a world which I regarded as a hostile place that was specifically anti-me.

For as long as I could remember I had been waging a guerrilla war against myself. For years I had been a dreamer, always imagining how things might have been *if only*. I accepted that the best in life would never come my way, that it was inconceivable to imagine myself as totally happy and content with what I had achieved, because in my state of passive hope I had achieved nothing worth shouting about. I deserved little and was simply lucky, I felt, and even that surprised me. But during that first stage of my recovery I quickly discovered that no amount of physical exercise or dietary improvement would benefit me unless I was able to break out of this sham world of twisted personal grievances. For as long as I remained in this state of passive hope, wishing and dreaming my life away from the sidelines, I could only expect to remain separated from what was going on around me and therefore indifferent to it. Life would continue to exclude me because I attached very little importance to most things that I did. I performed a list of daily functions like a pre-programmed robot, simply because it was expected of me.

For much of my life I had been clinging to the past, turning a deaf ear on the inner personality that screamed out in the silence of my depression: *Help me*! Yet for a long time I had known that there was little point in doing so, in nursing the ghosts and skeletons of a time that was now dead and useless. If I was ever going to go the final mile I needed to make a concerted effort to focus firmly, with all my energy, on the present, and from there move on to the future. In order to do that I had to take a serious look at another area of my life and change it radically: my values and my beliefs.

It was only when I sat down one evening early in my recovery period, once I had begun to feel a little better and sharper in my outlook, and made an effort to understand why I had been dreaming my way through some of the most important years of my life, that I realized *why* much of that life felt so flimsy and unimportant. The things I valued most about it seemed irrelevant. But just why did I value everything so little? Indeed, what exactly was this thing called a value that so many people regarded as being central and relevant to what it was they were trying to achieve in life?

For most of my young life I had believed that the values with which I was raised by my parents, and by my teachers and the priests and other figures of authority who influenced me then, were immutable absolutes, indelibly etched into my soul; no discussion or debate was entertained on these matters. These values were straightforward moral guidelines, simple explanations laid down by those in charge to help children cope with the more inexplicable areas of life. They related to things that we were brought up to believe were crucial in our lives, the very foundation of our happiness and well-being and, ultimately, our survival into adulthood. Education, hygiene, good living conditions, a proper moral outlook, good manners, respect for others – these were all intrinsic core values that shaped our childhood; to change these values would have been regarded as leaving my mind open to a darker, more unpredictable way of feeling and thinking that would cause me to veer right off course.

What no one told me then was that values related to one's goals in life, and that life would often throw up obstacles to force me to review my values and change them. At various times in life we reach a crossroads where we have to admit to ourselves that what we once valued and believed in no longer presents an accurate picture of us – we have become someone, or something, else. And conversely, sometimes these old values and beliefs prevent us from changing into what we must become if we are to continue to live happily and enjoy peace of mind.

My own childhood values fell apart when I was sexually abused. Up until that time I had always believed, as one of my core values, that priests and members of religious orders were special – unquestionably good, decent, holy people. How could I reconcile my values with what I had suffered at the hands of a man who was closer to God, my God, than I could ever expect to be myself? During my teenage years I was left with no values at all in some areas of my life, and as a result I regularly contemplated suicide.

Some years ago I debated with myself which came first in my life: goals or values. Most of the values that remained in me at that stage in my life, when I was on the cusp of starting out on my journey to recovery, felt flat and useless. I argued that, if these old values re-mained entrenched within me, my goals and outcomes would remain limited. I soon realized that, in order to discover what new values would direct my recovery, I must decide on the goals and outcomes that would make my life more fulfilling and contented. It made more sense to me to choose what I wanted to do before deciding on the values I needed in order to fulfil that outcome. It might seem like working backwards, but it worked for me.

Beliefs and goals go hand in hand. The single most important belief is *I can*. If I am able to look into the mirror and say honestly to myself, *I can*, then I will achieve my goal, which has to be *I will*. Once *I have*, I will have achieved my outcome. In order to be able to stand by my belief that *I can*, the new value must be well rooted deep within me.

At that stage I wanted to learn as much as I could about depression. If understanding was my desired outcome, then my value was going to be the importance of further education. My belief would be that I would find out as much as I could about depression. My goal was to pass whatever exams I needed to fulfil my outcome. The overall outcome would be that knowledge would finally overthrow my fear of relapsing into depression at some future date.

Values and beliefs need to be reviewed each time we go through one of life's major changes, whether it's a new job, the death of a loved one, separation and divorce, the birth of a child or a major illness. These are all events that create gigantic shifts at every level of our existence. At such times we adapt to different values and beliefs that become the new foundations in our lives, help us to handle these huge, often unexpected changes and encourage us to move on.

Depression is another of these huge life shifts, although inwardly we sufferers may feel stagnant and unable even to contemplate change. It is a demand made by the body–mind's inner systems to accept change, and to move in another direction if we are going to achieve the outcome that our deepest intuition is telling us we need. If our values and beliefs don't support this outcome we won't be able to put the goals in place, and we will never have the motivation we need to see those goals through and to achieve our desired end.

Many people who suffer from mid-life crises, the emotional uncertainty and confusion that come with reaching that point in life when we ask ourselves if this is really it, are often suffering from depression. This is precisely the way my own depression developed. I believed my wife no longer found me attractive. I felt alone and lonely, even though we lived in a noisy, happy home. At thirty-seven I had reached a point when I was asking myself that question: *is this it*? I couldn't imagine living like I had been living for another thirty years. I felt I had achieved nothing in life. I had no goals because I wasn't sure just what outcome I wanted to achieve. The reason for this was the outdated values and beliefs which dictated everything that happened – or, rather, didn't happen – in my life. I badly needed to know what outcome I wanted so that my life would seem worthwhile again; then I needed new values and beliefs, and a new goal, to support that outcome.

It's my belief that the main reason most of us are reluctant to change our values (apart from not knowing that we can if we want to) is that we are afraid of what other people will think of us and how we think they might react to our new values. This attitude has to go now if we are to succeed on our journey. The road ahead can only be exciting if we dare ourselves to be bold and different.

24

HELPING OTHERS

Ignorance is bliss: I have lost count of the number of times I have heard that famous – or should I say infamous – saying. Ignorance is also dangerous and very sad, and sadness cannot be described as blissful in any way. Knowledge, on the other hand, is power. To know is to conquer, and to learn is to become stronger and more committed. To become knowledgeable removes the fear from whatever it was that was making us afraid.

Depression arouses fear in most people. It's a condition that seems aloof and far-reaching, something that can't really be taken seriously enough to merit deliberate action, something that always defies logic, that can only be dealt with by psychiatrists and psychologists, something that inevitably destroys lives and the families of which its sufferers were once part. Yet it is also a topic on which most people choose to remain ignorant and detached. It's almost as if learning about this quite amazing combination of natural conditions will make a person susceptible to it themselves.

As part of my recovery I went back to college, where I studied a number of specific areas of psychology and behavioural science that I believed might help me to understand depression more clearly, and to get to the root of my own condition. But although it helped somewhat, I know now that no amount of study will help to overcome depression unless the studying starts within. My most effective form of study consisted of reaching an understanding of myself and of what was leading me to become depressed.

Since graduating and qualifying as a therapist and counsellor I have worked with many individuals who have suffered from depression, and with groups of medical staff who are involved in the field of mind health care. I enjoy the work because now I know what was wrong with me. In the same way that I came to understand my own crises and dilemmas, I now try to help others to understand that the solution to their depression lies within, and that that is where the healing process begins.

In order to recover and get beyond depression for ever, I tell people, they must have a creative idea of the type of person they badly want to become, and of the sort of life they badly want to live. I have deliberately used the word 'badly' twice here, because if you don't want it badly enough you will never get it. If we don't have an idea of what we want to be or of the life we crave, what is there to change into? This is just one of a list of seven useful guidelines which, I impress on people, are worth studying and absorbing at the kind of deep level that we usually reserve for our values and beliefs, so that ultimately they become second nature:

(1) Hating and resisting depression usually maintains it. Compassionate acceptance of our feelings and ourselves leads to freedom.

(2) We must detach from the past. Until we can do this, and begin to focus on the future, there will be no improvement in our lives.

(3) We must release all emotional scars, and stop storing old, painful 'baggage'.

(4) We must take control of every aspect of our conscious existence.

(5) We have to remember that we are not responsible for anyone else's happiness, just our own – in the same way that no one else is responsible for our happiness except ourselves.

(6) Real recovery involves intention. In order for us to be intent on success, we have to know what sort of person we want to become, and what sort of life we want to live.

(7) We must all live within what is possible – many people who win large sums of money suffer depression within a year!

In Chapter 15 I explained how essential it is for both sufferers and carers not to keep buttoned up about depression, but to take every opportunity to talk about it. Yet so many people find this impossible to do. One man told me he had always been reluctant to talk to his wife about her depression because he was afraid that bringing it out into the open might prompt her to kill herself. A woman told me she was afraid to discuss her son's depression with him because she thought she might have been partly responsible for the way he felt, and therefore felt guilty. Other people would desperately like to talk to someone outside their immediate family, to explain their problem and share their burden, but don't because they feel no one else will understand. They simply cannot bring themselves to broach the subject unless they are offered the encouragement of someone who has gone through the same experiences.

I was someone who had been through these experiences. I had made the journey successfully so far (and I say 'so far' consciously, because I believe this journey will continue for as long as I live), and it now seemed only right to give a helping hand to others who were looking for their right paths in life. Here are one or two of their stories.

Rita, in her late fifties, claimed she had been depressed for most of her adult life after losing her husband to another woman early in their marriage. She told me how her anger and resentment, and consequently her despair and helplessness, were too deep for her to reach.

I explained to her that they were not. She, and only she, had the capability to go to a deeper level still, to a level where only deep guided visual imagery and concentration could take her so that she could link up with her super-intelligence (or her soul, or her intuition – whatever she preferred to call it) and reverse the course of her illnesses, of which there were now many.

I taught her how to use guided visual imagery herself, and how to listen to the gaps between her thoughts – where the very soul of her being awaited her commands for change and the desire to take control once again. I showed her how to engage on this journey on a nightly basis, along with some gentle meditation, which enabled her to revisit the time when the shock of her ex-husband's news that he was leaving her created an emotional neuro-storm within her mind and body.

This storm of rage and distress had become 'stuck' in her mind and caused it to lock up. She had stopped living and remained frozen at just after the point in her life when her husband left her. Her immune system's 'mind' had similarly become frozen, stuck at the point when the crisis occurred. She called her depression a 'lame sad-ness'; at odd moments she was still expecting her hus-band to come home to her. Eventually we were able to unlock the hold these old emotions had on her, and enable her to move forward again.

A year later Rita was well, her depression now re-placed by hope, optimism and courage. She sent me a postcard to tell me she had managed to overcome her fear of flying and was off to visit her daughter in Melbourne where she would see her grandchildren for the first time in her life – now a proper life worth living again.

The story of another woman, Mary, shows how feel-ings need to be expressed openly and directly if joy is to reign supreme in our lives. She told me her life had fallen apart after her dog had been knocked down by a car and killed. Severely depressed, she said all she wanted was the happiness and security and peace of mind her little dog had given her when she was in her house alone at night. We spoke about getting her a replacement, but she explained it would be too painful to go through the experience again, knowing that the new dog might also die.

I knew she was still clinging to the old values, and that

unless she changed them her desired outcome, security and peace of mind, could never become reality. Joy would not get a look in without a change of direction. Eventually I convinced her it was for the best if she were to go out and get herself a new puppy. Reluctantly she agreed.

Within six weeks her depression had lifted, because she had achieved the outcome she wanted. 'The joy this little child of mine gives me is just indescribable,' she told me. The company of her friend had helped her to heal the pain of loss, and once again to experience the joy that her outcome had brought back into her life.

I have emphasized here and elsewhere how vital talking is to the understanding of depression, but it's not the only way to express how and what we feel. Crying is one of the purest and most honest forms of expression, yet many people are afraid to do so. It can be deeply upsetting for someone to see a loved one who is depressed crying inconsolably, but once they know that it's part of the healing process of self-expression, and not a sign that the condition is worsening, it becomes less painful and worrying to witness.

Patrick told me he couldn't bear to watch his wife crying all the time, that it was breaking his heart. She had been the boss in the house for as long as he could remember, he told me. She was also a nurse who, when she was well, had worked in a busy A&E department at the local hospital.

'She was always so strong, and now she's just helpless, crying and crying all the time,' he said.

I asked him whether he had cried with her.

'But surely that would only upset her more?' he replied in disbelief.

I shook my head. 'I don't see why. You love her. She loves you. She's been strong for you all her life, so much so that you weren't aware of it at times. Now she needs you to be strong for her, and if that means crying, then cry. It's a way of telling her that it's OK to cry and that you are hurting for her, instead of leaving the room whenever she starts to get tearful. The only reason you walk away is because you're afraid you're going to start crying as well. Don't be afraid. Cry with her. Put on her favourite song. Hold her hands tightly. Let her put her arms around you and wipe her tears on your shoulder. I guarantee, if you do that she won't be depressed for too long and you'll both love each other a hundred times more strongly.'

He left me looking stunned and bemused.

But it worked. He called me a few months later to tell me she had gone back to her job at the hospital and was doing really well. They were holding hands every-where they went – the first time in over fifteen years that they had felt, and shown, such intimacy towards each other.

What Patrick was doing was expressing his love in a way that was truly meaningful in the context of his wife's depression. When someone tells you they love you unexpectedly, the surge of emotions is almost unbear-able. It is my belief that if each of us was to hear the words 'I love you', spoken genuinely and empathetically three times a day, every day, we would all live longer, stronger, more hopeful and more fruitful lives. Love is the enemy of hatred and self-loathing, the greatest weapon in battles of any kind, the opponent of war and strife, and the primary, most singularly effective antidote to depression.

25

THE LEARNING CURVE

I have learned more about life – about me and who I really am – in the last three years than I did in the previous thirty-nine. Then again, maybe those thirty-nine years were gearing me up for this second chance to discover who I really am. My healing started within days of a diagnosis three years ago, and I expect that process to continue for another thirty – more if I am lucky enough to live longer. Healing is a part of living, and to heal fully takes for ever. To heal depression is to become aware of exactly who I am, of what in life I am capable of becoming so that the healing present me with new opportunities.

Initially I wanted my medication to 'cure' me. I needed it to do all the spadework for me, and it didn't because it couldn't. That, for me, was the point when my healing started in earnest. I became the architect, even though I wasn't sure what I was meant to be designing. It was a terrifying, isolating experience to undertake such a challenge, but in hindsight I know I didn't need to feel such terror. I allowed my intuition to guide me, and it has never let me down.

What does still terrify is to recall how close I came to killing myself and thus to depriving myself of the incredible discoveries I have made over the past three years about myself, my life and my capabilities. It's been incredibly tough, let's make no mistake about that; but it has worked for me and I am so pleased I stayed alive to savour the success and joy of my achievements.

Parents get very nervous when their twelve-year-old sons and daughters ask questions like, 'What's the point in being alive when life is so horrible?' or 'Why do I feel like killing myself some days?' I know I regularly asked myself these questions when I was a young boy – I was afraid to ask them out loud for fear my parents might think the worst and send me for a psychiatric evaluation. These are highly charged, extremely upsetting questions, and most of the time it's difficult for mothers and fathers to find accurate and acceptable answers to them. To start with, any parent is going to be knocked back by the power of such seemingly negative sentiments, as they might instinctively interpret them.

The truth is there is nothing wrong with asking such invaluable questions, no matter how young or mature, how well developed or well balanced, you might think you are. Asking a question like, 'What's the point in being alive when life is so horrible?' is only like asking, 'What can I do with my life that might raise me above the level of living that seems to be dragging me down all the time?' It might be difficult for a twelve-year-old to change his life radically, but it can be crucial to his future happiness to understand that the life stretching out ahead of him is a map on which he can mark the outcomes he wants that will make his life as worthwhile as he would like it to be. I know now that this question formed the core of my depressed state. If only I could have found an answer to that question my depression would not have hurt me so painfully.

So just what have I learned about the 'wounded child' that I kept at a distance, shut out in the cold for over thirty years? I've learned so much about him – or perhaps he has taught me so much about my life, which is also his life.

I enjoy his company greatly now. I love him. He's kind and soft-hearted, genuine and honest, and speaks the truth about the way he feels. He's striving every day to be a better father to his three beautiful daughters, Kerri, Katie and Aibhin, who were hugely instrumental in his recovery. He's very proud of his achievements, something he could never cope with being in past years.

He's also discovered that his boredom threshold has dropped dramatically, and that he doesn't suffer fools gladly any longer (and maybe that's not a bad thing). He's far more assertive (and a little cranky at times, but hey! No one's perfect). He's stronger in more ways than he can count, and he loves the opportunity to reach out to others who he instantly recognizes are going through the living hell and life-shattering experience he became so familiar with himself.

I am different in all these ways and more, but, strangely, I am also still the same. I just allow myself to experience things differently, the way I now want to see them. I accept my past as part of who I have become today, not as part of the person I used to hate and feel contempt and shame for. The abuse I suffered as a young boy doesn't interfere with my life any more, and I have forgiven the man who was responsible.

I am still quite shy and retiring, and prefer to listen rather than to speak – although I've also learned that I can be the loudest, most assertive voice in the room if I need to be. It's in the art of listening that we discover the gift of awareness and the promise of hope. There are times when my mind still tries to crowd me out, with its non-stop thinking and arguing and questioning, but I'm a good match for it now.

I know now that the qualities that attract me to others and connect me into new relationships, whether at work or in my private life, are very different from what might have attracted me to people in the past. I want to reach out to the people I like to be surrounded by so that my effect on their lives will be as positive as their effect on mine. I have also discovered, to my surprise, that I can enjoy my own company at last. So often in the past the thought of being alone terrified me. Now I think of it as the art of solitude, and occasionally after a busy week relish the notion of tucking myself away with a good book, a glass of wine and a tinge of nostalgia on the CD player. It doesn't take much to please me now; but then again, it's all back down to simplicity, which gives me room to admire the view.

I used to worry that my years of emotional turmoil might affect my daughters, especially the eldest, Kerri, who was reaching an impressionable age when I was going through hell and showing it. I feared that the confusion and anger and distance she witnessed in her father might leave scars that would affect her in later life. So I have tried to help her to understand that we all go through difficult times while trying to reach the real self that we are on the inside. I see so much of me in her make-up, in her softly quiet temperament and her good humour, just like I can sense so many aspects of my personality, my values and my beliefs, in my other girls. A day never passes without me telling them how much I love them. I cling to my family. They are my life. With them I know I am whole and complete.

I hope that all the weird and wonderful things I have learned about who I am from the experiences I endured will help others in their search to find out who they really are and what they want. The choice will always be mine, as I remind myself here of the days when it seemed easier to crawl back under the duvet and close my eyes to shield them from the bright sunshine that snaked through the crack in the drawn curtains, on those warm yet strange summer afternoons when my daughters hoped that maybe Daddy might come downstairs today and play with them in the garden beneath my bedroom window. Now I do. The choice is mine.

26

THE CHALLENGE OF THE FUTURE

To recover means 'to bring back', but that was not what I wanted to do. Another meaning for it is 'to succeed in reaching'. This is what my recovery was about, as it should be for anybody who is suffering from depression. I wanted to succeed in reaching a new level of my life, within what was possible, beyond the old routines and destructive habits. This is true recovery. I have already stated that, having come a long way on this journey of recovery, I believe I will not become depressed again. This is something I tend to mention when I give talks to groups of people on the subject of depression and recovery; often hands go up and someone will inevitably ask me how I can be so sure.

What I have managed to do is *diffuse* my depression. I like that word 'diffuse' – it means, literally, to 'pour out all around'. It's like another way of describing the ability to express how we feel. For me it meant lessening the oppressiveness I felt in my darkest days, when the invisible knot seemed to tighten enough to suffocate me. By diffusing my depression, I made it too weak to have any real adverse effect on me. I became free.

Like everyone, I have bad days. No matter how well we do or how well we feel, we are all going to have to deal with low moods and bad days and difficult situations that might throw us and remind us of the very bad days – but that is not depression. Up to three years ago I could never have handled and mastered a bad day. One bad day simply slipped into another, until I was generally having a bad time, and eventually the bad time became a severely depressing period with no beginning, no middle and no end.

Today is different. There are moments when I feel that familiar icy grip on my shoulder from somewhere in the distant past. It usually comes when I am feeling over-stressed or angry, moody or indecisive – all the states of mind that contributed to my depression over the years. Then I have to issue a reminder that I am allowing myself to slip into these unwanted states of mind. I have to tell myself that I have *chosen* to get angry with whoever or whatever it is, or to become indecisive instead of standing firm and making the decision.

Again, this is not depression, which is why I say categorically that I won't be allowing myself to become depressed again. This is a rule, or a principle, that each of us who has experienced depression must build up and become part of over a period of time; it goes hand in hand with this journey that we have set out on. It's too simplistic just to say that I don't want to be depressed. Suffering from depression isn't like suffering from flu or a bad migraine; it's far more complex and involves a far greater personal input. After all, I got myself into this situation. There's no point in saying to a doctor, 'Get me out of here!' He can't. I can – and only I.

Once I stopped being afraid of my depression, once I had faced up to this journey and seen it as that rather than as a slow, methodical, painful recovery process, my perception of life started to change for the better. And with that change came a stronger realization of what I needed to do with my life based on what I wanted to get out of it.

At the time of writing I am forty-two. I like to think I am only halfway through this journey called life. I have been writing my own destiny script for the past three years, and the experience is wonderfully empowering. Working through depression, moving beyond it and finding your true inner self, can be an impossible task, but it is a choice that every single person who suffers from this strange condition has to make. Alternatively it can be the most enlightening, invigorating and exhilarating experience that you will ever go through in your whole life. *Do I move on*, you must ask yourself, *or do I stay still and die?*

One year after the disaster that robbed them of their loved ones, the families of the *Challenger* space shuttle crew collectively issued a powerful statement: 'Do not fear risk. All exploration, all growth is calculated. Without challenge people cannot reach their higher selves. Only if we are willing to walk over the edge can we become winners.' The only people who have gone on in life to achieve amazing outcomes are those who dared to believe that something inside them was greater and more magnificent and more powerful than the external circumstances that other people allow to pull them down. Depression, despite its horrors and its unpredictability, gives each one of us an amazing opportunity to change what people regard as the unchangeable; to examine and restructure and mould what many people don't even know exists.

I no longer see this as a long, hard road that I am struggling along; now I regard it as a journey of discovery, at times exciting, at other times confusing and exhausting – but that's fine. It's a journey that I can take my time over, not needing to rush if I don't want to, not needing to do anything I don't want to. 'Stick with the winners' is an expression my father regularly uses. For years it made no sense to me because I never regarded myself as a winner. But a winner is not necessarily the person who crosses the finishing line first; he may be the person who cheers you from the sideline as you get closer to your own chosen goal. Winners always give me hope. They tell me I can do it, without having to say anything to me. Now I know that we are all winners.

One of the strange ironic truths about depression is that the healing takes place when we concentrate on the present and future, not on the past. It doesn't matter how we yearn for the past, or try to revisit it; that's where it will all remain, unchanged and unchanging. It will always be behind us. Whenever, during my years of depression, I looked back at the past I always used to feel powerless and lost because nothing could be changed, or erased, or forgotten. I used to think that if I could just re-create the past for a brief second my depression would no longer affect me or hurt me. It wasn't true, of course. And, paradoxically, the thought alone was making me even more depressed, making me hate the present and dread the future, which during the brief respites from my worst periods of depression used to terrify me. Nowadays I revel in the idea of the future and all its possibilities. When I look to the future today I think to myself: *You have the power to do anything you want.*

FURTHER READING

Here's a small selection of the books I've read and been inspired by over the last few years. Most of them are what I would call 'reader-friendly' and are available in most good bookstores; sadly, some of those listed are now out of print. However, there are a number of excellent websites where many of these older books can be tracked down quite easily, including Amazon and Barnes & Noble (bn.com). These were usually my first port of call when I found books difficult to locate.

Alborn, Mitch, *Tuesdays with Morrie*, Little, Brown, 1997

Awbrey, David S., *Finding Hope in the Age of Melancholy*, Little, Brown, 1999

Benson, Herbert, M.D., *Timeless Healing: The Power and Biology of Belief*, Simon & Schuster, 1996

Bradshaw, John, *Healing the Shame that Binds You*, Health Communications Inc, 1988

Braun, Stephen, *The Science of Happiness: Unlocking the Mysteries of Mood*, Wiley, 2000

Breggin, Peter R., M.D., and Cohen, David, Ph.D., *Your Drug May Be Your Problem*, Perseus, 2000

Chopra, Deepak M.D., *Perfect Health: The Complete Mind Body Guide*, Bantam, 2001

Covey, Stephen R., *The 7 Habits of Highly Effective People*, Simon & Schuster, 1992

De Mello, Anthony, *Awareness*, Fount, 1997

Eadie, Barry J., *Embraced by the Light*, Bantam, 1994

Epstein Rosen, Laura, Ph.D., and Amador, Xavier Francisco, Ph.D., *When Someone You Love Is Depressed*, Simon & Schuster, 1997

Frankl, Viktor E., *Man's Search for Meaning*, Washington Square Press, 1985

Hansard, Christopher, *The Tibetan Art of Living*, Hodder & Stoughton, 2001

Hedaya, Robert J. M.D., *The Anti-Depressant Survival Program: How to Beat the Side Effects and Enhance the Benefits of Your Medication*, Crown, 2000

Hutschnecker, Arnold A. M.D., *Hope: The Dynamics of Self-Fulfilment*, Putnam, 1981

Lynch, Terry, M.D., *Beyond Prozac: Healing Mental Suffering Without Drugs*, Marino, 2001

O'Connor, Richard, Ph.D., *Undoing Depression: What Therapy Doesn't Teach You and Medication Can't Give You*, Berkeley, 1997

Pert, Candace B. Ph.D., *Molecules of Emotion: Why You Feel the Way You Feel*, Simon & Schuster, 1998

Rowe, Dorothy, *Depression: The Way out of Your Prison*, Routledge, 1999

Siegel, Bernie M.D., *Love, Medicine and Miracles*, Harper Perennial, 1990

Smith, Jeffery, *Where the Roots Reach for Water: A Personal & Natural History of Melancholia*, North Point Press, 1999

Solomon, Andrew, *The Noonday Demon*, Chatto & Windus, 2001

Stoll, Andrew L. M.D., *The Omega-3 Connection*, Simon & Schuster, 2001

Vale, Jason, *Slim 4 Life: Freedom From the Food Trap*, Thorsons, 2002

Watts, Terence, *Warriors, Settlers and Nomads*, Crown House, 2000